ORIGINS OF A
SOUTHERN MOSAIC

ORIGINS

OF A

SOUTHERN

MOSAIC

*Studies of
Early Carolina and
Georgia*

CLARENCE L. VER STEEG

*MERCER UNIVERSITY LAMAR
MEMORIAL LECTURES, NO. 17*

THE UNIVERSITY OF GEORGIA PRESS

ATHENS

©

1975

THE UNIVERSITY OF GEORGIA PRESS

Library of Congress Catalog Card Number: 74–18587

International Standard Book Number: 0–8203–0365–8

Printed in the United States of America

To Dorothy

Contents

Foreword

When Mrs. Eugenia Dorothy Blount Lamar established the memorial lectures at Mercer University she doubtless intended that they cover the whole breadth and scope of southern history and culture from the beginning. For various reasons most of the lectures have been studies of the nineteenth and twentieth centuries. Not since Bernard Mayo, the second lecturer of the series, has attention been largely focused on colonial history or personages.

Anxious to redress this imbalance and very much aware of the approaching bicentennial of the American Revolution, the Lamar Memorial Lectures Committee began to turn to early American historians. The committee was fortunate in being able to bring to the Mercer campus Clarence L. Ver Steeg, professor of history at Northwestern University and a noted colonial scholar. It was a source of great pleasure to all that Professor Ver Steeg chose to devote much attention in his lectures to the origins of the colony of Georgia. The present volume thus marks an auspicious beginning of the celebration leading to 1776 and beyond. As the bicentennial approaches, other well-known specialists in early American history will visit the campus and their lectures will be added to the growing list of Lamar publications.

Professor Ver Steeg's reputation as a colonial historian preceded him to the Mercer campus by many years. His publications, including much southern history, are innumerable, and more are happily expected. He has served the historical and educational professions in many posts, including that of chairman of the executive committee of the Institute of Early American History and Culture. His talent for research and his genius for extrapolating ideas will be readily apparent in this volume to both laymen and scholars. Of especial interest are his conclusions about precisely why Georgia and the Carolinas developed as they did (or did not), and his comments on the origins and economics of the Carolina slave system deserve close attention. Professor Ver Steeg's success as a lecturer was delightfully demonstrated when at the end of his second lecture a member of the audience spontaneously called out, "Why did you stop so soon?"

Eugenia Dorothy Blount Lamar (1867–1955) was a prominent, civic-minded middle Georgian who sought to preserve the values of southern culture by creating and endowing the annual Lamar Memorial Lectures. Her faith and farsightedness have been more than justified. Professor Ver Steeg's contribution, the seventeenth in the series, continues unbroken the high level of scholarship called for in Mrs. Lamar's will.

This printed edition of four lectures is an expanded form of the original three lectures delivered on the Macon, Georgia, campus of Mercer University, 25 and 26 March 1974.

Henry Y. Warnock
Lamar Memorial Lectures Committee

Mercer University
Macon, Georgia

Preface

No one living in the southern United States of today
or in the colonies founded along the Atlantic coastline south
of Pennsylvania need be told his region is not or was not a
monolith. Daily experience taught them otherwise. The rich
composition of peoples, places, occupations, speech, background, and cultures can match that of most if not all parts
of the nation. Yet the concept of "the South" commands sufficient specificity in the minds of Americans that the term
is used with confidence by everyone—politicians and busi-
nessmen, writers and scholars, teachers and students.

But what does the term "the South" connote? A geo-
graphical area? an attitude? a state of mind? linguistic pe-
culiarities? a distinctive character and culture? Politicians
have spoken of a southern strategy, not always using that
precise term, for more than a century and a half, and courses
on the South have been offered in universities since historians developed a professional curriculum. Shelves bend under the weight of books on the South. If the South exists,
when did it originate and what were or are its characteristics?

In the late seventeenth and early eighteenth centuries,
New England could be identified as a distinctive region because of the shared background in England of most of its
settlers, its religious ideas and practices, its method of granting land, and its common considerations of governance. In
exploring each of these elements, the colonies south of
Pennsylvania stand in stark contrast. The development of

each was distinct, individual, and separate. Virginia, settled by English Anglicans seeking profit and adventure, was the legacy of a bankrupt joint-stock company. Maryland emerged from a bargain the king struck with the Baltimore family. As a proprietorship its government and its method of granting lands did not correspond with the practices of Virginia, and its settlement by Catholics and Protestants represented an almost unbridgeable difference. The early history of the Carolinas had no link with Virginia or Maryland. The background of the people who settled in the Carolinas, the government under which they lived, and the crops they produced had little if anything in common with the colonists in Virginia or Maryland. Georgia was a unique experiment in the history of English colonization. Yet these colonies, differing so dramatically in character, are the antecedents of what we label the American South.

The essays presented in this volume are an attempt to address the problem of delineating the origins of the American South. It is not begging the issue, in my judgment, to suggest that one of the bonds that define the South is its quilt-like mosaic, identifiable enclaves that contribute a special quality to the whole. For the purposes of illustration, I have limited my focus to early South Carolina and Georgia and examined various representative facets to explain why they developed as they did. My approach is selective, not comprehensive. Obviously, the lectures as delivered were abstracted from these essays.

The opportunity to offer my ideas in such a congenial setting as the Lamar Lectures made the event itself a memorable one. Contributing to this result were Professor Spencer B. King, Jr., Professor Henry Y. Warnock, their departmental colleagues at Mercer University, and the Lamar Memorial Lectures Committee. The warm response of the audience on that occasion encourages me to believe that my effort to illuminate the historical issues involving the origin and development of the American South can contribute to a broader intellectual debate.

Clarence L. Ver Steeg

Northwestern University

ORIGINS OF A
SOUTHERN MOSAIC

ONE

The Political Background of Proprietary Carolina:

Fraction Is the Calculus of the Tymes

IN 1690 JOHN STEWART, A RESIDENT OF SOUTH CAROLINA AND a partisan politico, wrote to a friend in Scotland: "Thus fraction fraction is the Calculus of the Tymes." [1] And so it was. Between 1690 and 1700 six men occupied the office of governor in South Carolina, resulting in seven separate administrations: James Colleton, 1686–1690; Seth Sothell, 1690–1691; Philip Ludwell, 1691–1693; Thomas Smith, 1693–1694; Joseph Blake, 1694; John Archdale, 1694–1696; and Joseph Blake, 1696–1700. Because each governor—if his brief term permitted—appointed a deputy for North Carolina, its record of administrative change resembles that of South Carolina. Despite these frequent turnovers in the governor's office, the underlying political themes remained remarkably consistent: between 1690 and 1700 the politics of South Carolina was dominated by a successful effort on the part of the colonists to gain ascendancy in making policy at the expense of the power of the proprietors, a development that was delayed more than a decade in North Carolina. With colonial control firmly established in South Carolina by 1700, the political focus changed, and a new question was posed: Which group within the colony was to have the preeminent voice in the determination of policy? [2]

I

In 1690 South Carolina was on the brink of political convulsion. James Colleton, brother of one of the proprietors, Sir Peter Colleton, had held the office of governor since 1686. He was confronted with a general intransigence, because Carolinians, constituting a broad spectrum of political opinions, held him responsible for the stalemate that had developed in public policy. Rumors, largely unsubstantiated, had reached the colony that French and Spanish forces were advancing on the settlement, but the governor refused to convene the legislature. Colonial leaders were torn between supporting the governor in the face of a possible common enemy or abandoning Colleton altogether, preferring to meet whatever crisis arose unencumbered with an executive whose rigid, legalistic approach exacerbated problems rather than eased them and who commanded the loyalty of only a narrow band of supporters.[3]

In a pamphlet written in 1690, John Stewart, an ardent Colleton man, whose ambition outstripped his modest role as small planter–Indian trader, attempted to make a case for the governor. The governor's opponents, he observed, were party men, self-interested conspirators, led by a colonial "Matchivell," unidentified but doubtlessly Job Howes (often spelled "How" by contemporaries), who had been a leader of the opposition in the last meeting of the assembly. These men, Stewart explained, planned and schemed "to blow up the parliament," not literally, of course, but by doing nothing while pretending to protect the security of Carolina. Meanwhile, asserted Stewart, the strategy of Governor Colleton's opponents was to leak incriminating information: "The pigmy dwarfy narrow scanty soull cannot containe its own tho-w-ghts or measurs but here and there a little scatters, which evry warty and prudent ear sucks up." Adversaries of the governor, in turn, declared that he "betray'd his trust to the Lords," that he acted outside his instructions, and that, as a result, "al the measurs of Government and evry single step thereof that he had made use of for 3 years were bot [but] mushroum ordinances and Illegall Laws, yea disloyall traiterous and treacherous both to the K. [King] and Lds. [Lord Proprietors]." [4]

The position taken by Colleton's opponents taxed the limits of Stewart's pejorative vocabulary. "How monstruous and stupendious a pice of Jugle [deceit] it wes [was]." With no less than the security of the colony at stake,

> Such Meanders of Ruining polecies . . . undermind our Goshen exposing the province designedly to ruine and Calamity by a french conquest, that we had vipers in our own in our bowels gnawing the commonwealth in pices and fractions, cary'd on by Jehu-like driving Jehu-like on a designe that contradicts and gives itself the lye in all its pretensions. . . . And this pernicious wheill [wheel] of politicks unskilfully lays open the very nervs and sinews, muscles and arteries of once seeming politicall bot now a . . . fatuus Trap.

But the polemic was not at an end. "Ar the Inhabitants blinded, can they not sie bot a charme and Infatuatione from the pestiferous breath of a Jugling Tongue has almost bro-w-ght the Country on the brink of Ruine and hazard, and dayly we lie open to all the Insults and Calamitys that warr from Papists may offer or Impose." [5]

Job Howes was etched in black. "Had Raphael Angelo or Albertus Durer," the latter especially known for his somber paintings, "with a pencill been at work to have drawn this Hydra viperous Monster of politicks a worser never affrick [Africa] bredd." According to Stewart, he challenged Howes with swordplay: "We standing 6 minuts with sword to sword 2 foot within other," but Howes, "the cowardly roage [rogue]," according to Stewart, suggested that they sheath their weapons. When Stewart finally agreed to terminate this confrontation and started to move off, a friend of Howes clutched Stewart's arm while Howes "cam up basely and struck me with a hickory stick." Stewart, according to his own account, wrenched himself free, swung his sword, and "mist my stroak within an Inch of his [Howes's] neck," which sent the latter scampering off.[6]

Whatever the results of this match may have been, Stewart claimed that his written word won a favorable hearing among leading Carolinians. "The Governor wes [was] pleas'd, when I first read it to him befor a Company of his friends [*sic*], to say it wes the best and sharpest and truest to the text that ev'r he heard or read in his lyfetyme of that nature." Such admiration from Colleton was not surprising, but Stewart claimed broader support: Captain Robert Quary, a former governor dismissed for allegedly consorting with pirates, and, reputedly, a committed opponent of Colleton in the past; Ralph Izard, a more moderate critic; and Joseph Blake, also a former governor. More significant is Stewart's claim of a favorable reception from Captain James Moore, a hearty self-serving spirit whose fame in the colony had yet to reach its zenith. Even Maurice Mathews, called "the prince" by Stewart and whose contest against Colleton was a matter of record in the last assembly, appeared to waiver, especially when Nathaniel Johnson, a prosperous planter and former governor of the Leeward Islands who recently arrived to settle in Carolina, seemed favorably disposed toward Colleton.[7]

But the governor, inclined to respond to a crisis with fixed solutions and prodded by a few of his confidants, particularly Thomas Smith, a deputy and landgrave, and Paul Grimball, described by a contemporary as "hot and martial" and the "Eyesore to the party" and even acknowledged by the proprietors to be a man of "indiscretion," invoked martial law. This step was taken after more than one hundred men signed a petition requesting it. In later recantations some who signed declared that they were misinformed and misled. Certainly, the governor's friends misinterpreted the initial response to martial law. Those who opposed the petition, according to Stewart, were merely "wasps of the party" who were "at Work to dam further subscriptions to the petition." Indeed, with martial law, "we overcom all opposition and laid flat all their desynes [designs]." Tranquility blossomed, he remarked, because of "a Lock on all the party's tongues." [8]

Scorning criticism of the consequence of the martial law, Stewart raised a question: "fears from the ffrench hes [has] been hush't and suppres't bot fears and jealousies of a Councell of Warr hes bine presented in a Magnifying Glas, Insomuch that a bussy party hes held furth greater dainger and loss . . . from a councell and Jury of its own Inhabitants then from forayne Enemyes that ar [are] papists[.] If the Countrys Militia doe bot ordinary dewty will their own Nighbors and Inhabitants ruine them?" [9]

The penultimate act of the governor, declaring martial law on the pretense of protecting the colony from foreign encroachment when his primary goal was to safeguard his personal power, inadvertently gave the antiproprietary men enough leverage eventually to overthrow his administration and to set a course toward a final rejection of proprietary rule. Colleton discovered that martial law can only be enforced with militia, that militia are composed of settlers, and that settlers hesitate to take action against themselves. Invoking martial law, rather than placing "a Lock on all the party's Tongues," as asserted by Stewart, raised resentment that solidified colonial leadership against Colleton, the proprietor's representative. When Seth Sothell, who had become a proprietor by purchasing the share of Lord Clarendon, arrived in Charleston, some five hundred petitioners, representing a broad spectrum of political views and every geographic sector as well as including many of the principal men in the colony, forced the overturn of Colleton and the elevation of Sothell.[10]

II

The issues dividing the partisans were of long standing. In a petition to Sothell, drawn up by Governor Colleton's critics, the colonial position was defined in incisive language.

On the distribution of land and its cost, the collection of quitrents, and the procedure to be followed to obtain grants, proprietary policy not only failed to satisfy the Carolinians, but in certain of its consequences, they asserted, deceived them.

> We, in behalfe of the whole Countrey, most humbly and heartily begg and beseech the Lords Proprietors out of their favorable beneficence to be pleased to grant that whatever the conveyance be that the Lands shall therein be granted for a penny an acre or the vallew [value] thereof, without any expressed reservation of re-entry, & the people will allwayes, in parliment or otherwise, be ready to adjust the price of Comodityes, so as that the Lords Proprietors shall be gainers, and then we doubt not but in a very few years to see such multitudes of tennants here as that their Lordships shall quickly be re-imbursed their great charge.[11]

On the Indian trade: "But in this case, as in all other publick actions, an endeavour was made, upon pretence of this Law, to stopp all persons from going abroad to trade with the Indians, while the late Governor [Colleton] was providinge to send himselfe, and did, allsoe, after a little time, goe in his owne person out of the Settlement, and commanded agen, as formerly, noe [no] Yamassee Indian to goe and assist any man in trading but himselfe, and then sent people to trade, &c." [12]

When Colleton became governor, he removed a number of officials from office with the approval of the proprietors.

These men, Robert Quary being one, were among the principals who prepared the petition, and their disgruntlement pervades the document:

> That the Deputies and other Magistrates and Officers, Civill and Military, have been every day put out and others put in, without any respect to their qualityes, parts, honesty or other abilityes, and the Commoners of the Grand Council turned out, under pretence of misdemeanour, for any unwary action or word committed or said out of Councill or over a bottle of wine in a taverne; and this hath been and may still be done with ease, for there is but eight Commoners [delegates of the electorate in the assembly] when all the places are full (which seldome happens of late yeares)[;] and if one of the Deputies charge one of them with any action or word, misdone or said, the person accused must stand by, and then there is eight Deputies to vote against seaven Commoners, which, not onely in this case but in all others, make the Grand Councill which is alsoe all Courts of Justice, except the County Court, and receive, allsoe, appealls from that, be wholy in all its Judgments, Acts, Orders and Ordinances as the Governor and Deputyes please,[;] and they not onely have a negative but an affirmative upon all occasions, and to justifye all this doe record the matters as they please and have entred men present when absent, &c., as we are ready to prove.[13]

The longest and most exacting segment of the petition was reserved for an opening statement, providing a detailed recital of the history of the Fundamental Constitutions as proposed by proprietors and the respective colonial responses to those initiatives.

> That the methods which those principally entrusted by the Lords Proprietors have, for many yeares, used for the imposition of the seaverall fundamentall Constitutions afore mentioned, have caused much uneasiness and trouble to the good Inhabitants of this Countrey in generall and many persons in particular, have felt upon the least surmised occasion the indignation, rather then [*sic*] the justice, of those that governe here,[;] and many thousands of people have

been detered from cominge hither to the disconsolation of
those that are here, & the disprofitt of the Lords Proprietors[;] and many alsoe left the Cuntrey, being not willinge
to live constantly after soe uncertaine and unquiett a rate.[14]

The petition was addressed to Seth Sothell who assumed
the office of governor under a provision in the Fundamental
Constitutions which authorized a proprietor in residence
to become governor. Sothell's appearance as a knight to res-
cue distressed colonists in South Carolina was tinged with
irony, for only a few months earlier he had left a situation in
Albemarle (North Carolina) in which he had been accused
of using his authority as the proprietary representative ar-
bitrarily. Petitions written by Albemarle colonials to the
proprietors in England accused Sothell of gross misdeeds:
confiscation of land held by political opponents, the impris-
onment of individuals under false charges, and taking
bribes. There is evidence to modify, if not to doubt, the hue
and cry of the petitioners. Before coming to Albemarle,
Sothell was regarded as a man of moderation; and, it should
be noted, the petitioners were not only Sothell's political
opponents, but precisely those men who, assuming the
powers of government in the absence of a representative
from the proprietors, had everything their own way—until
Sothell arrived. Sothell was relieved of his office in North
Carolina by his fellow proprietors, and Philip Ludwell, appointed governor-elect of North Carolina in his place, was
instructed to determine whether the complaints against
Sothell were justified.[15]

These proprietary orders and appointments, obviously at
odds with events as they transpired, were still circulating
in the unreliable transatlantic communication system; the
pressing problems at Charleston required immediate action.
Whatever is said of Sothell at Albemarle, his conduct at
Charleston won broad support among the colonists. Because
of a peculiar situation resulting from the dispute with Colle-

ton, Carolina, in relation to its legislation and law, could begin with a clean slate. A provision in the Fundamental Constitutions specified that any enactment was automatically terminated at the end of two years if not renewed by the Carolina Parliament or ratified by the proprietors and thereupon published at the following session of Parliament. When Colleton refused to call a meeting of the Carolina Parliament new measures were not enacted and the old ones expired. Consequently, when Sothell became governor no statutes were legally in force.

The new governor summoned the Carolina Parliament, which adopted some forty statutes covering a broad range of issues critical to the colony: regulation of the Indian trade, establishment of a system of courts, rules to govern the issuance of licenses, provision for militia, regulation and improvement of inland transportation, confirming political and civil rights of freeborn citizens upon French protestants, an election law, and other needed legislation. In a colony with an unenviable history of contention, the preparation and acceptance of these statutes in so short a time constituted a genuine achievement.[16]

The enactment of an extensive legislative program is seldom attained without political cost. In the case of Sothell, his actions were bitterly opposed by proprietary-appointed officeholders in Carolina who posted notices throughout the province that instructed colonists to defy Sothell; in England Sothell's fellow proprietors, upon learning of his actions, censured him. Paul Grimball, who received his appointment as secretary of the colony under Governor Colleton from the proprietors, refused to turn over his records and the Great Seal of the colony to Sothell, whereupon the governor seized the records by force and imprisoned Grimball. Perhaps the tenacity and impertinance of these few diehard Colleton men, together with the confidence engendered in Sothell by his seemingly sweeping popular mandate, entrapped the new governor in acts of retribution for which he was held responsible. He participated in the passage of punitive legislation that barred Colleton from Carolina and excluded forever many of Colleton's appointees from holding public office. The unseated governor was directed to appear in England to defend himself against formal charges as yet unformulated. Although this legislation was much less the result of an arbitrary decision by Sothell than an act of vengeance sought by leaders in the Carolina Parliament, the enactments were imprudent if not downright witless, because they set the proprietors in England against Sothell.[17]

The proprietors invalidated the laws enacted during Governor Sothell's brief term of office and declared that his conduct was not only illegal but so offensive as to constitute a high misdemeanor and even treason. In their view, the governor, in a quaint phrase, was "outing of the rest of the proprietors of their Rights." It is likely that Sothell, since he was not one of the established proprietary families, was resented by his colleagues in England. Moreover, the fact that the deposed Governor Colleton was the brother of proprietor Sir Peter Colleton did nothing to aid the Sothell case.[18]

In any event, Sothell was removed from office on the basis of the extraordinary official argument that the Fundamental Constitutions, because of the failure of the Carolinians to accept them, made his appeal to its provisions obsolete. Only the specifications of the charter, it was asserted, prevailed. Under its provisions, a new governor was appointed —Philip Ludwell of Virginia and more recently Sothell's successor in North Carolina—who had married the widow of William Berkeley, late governor of Virginia and one of the original proprietors of Carolina.[19]

The administration of Philip Ludwell is significant solely

because during his tenure the issues involved in the confrontation between the proprietors and the colonists were more sharply defined; eventually the power of the proprietors was diminished and that of the Carolinians strengthened. After the dismissal of Sothell, the proprietary officials in the colony, regardless of the strategy or tactics they employed, simply could not escape this course of events. To trace the struggle in detail would, in itself, involve a small volume; yet it is essential to indicate the broad outlines, using as a preeminent case study the response of the colonials to the Fundamental Constitutions as the basis for governance.

III

So much has been said about the Fundamental Constitutions, originally drafted in 1669 to serve as the organic act of the new colony, and yet much remains to be written. The idea that the Fundamental Constitutions was a wild scheme, wholly inapplicable to a New World and therefore to be discarded as inconsequential, has fortunately been thoroughly discredited by recent studies. Although never accepted in its entirety, the Fundamental Constitutions influenced Carolina land policy and religious development, to a degree its social structure, and certainly its government, especially that of North Carolina.[20]

Scholars are generally in agreement regarding the circumstances surrounding the preparation of the Fundamental Constitutions. A clause, common to many colonial charters, is found in the Carolina Charter of 1665: "And because such Assemblies of Freeholders cannot be so suddenly called as there may be occasion to require the same: We do . . . give and Grant . . . full power and authority, from time to time, to make and Ordain fit and wholesome

Orders and Ordinances, within the Province or Territory aforesaid . . . to be kept and observed . . . for the better Government of the People there abiding." [21]

Acting accordingly, the proprietors adopted the Fundamental Constitutions, a document prepared principally by Lord Ashley, one of the most influential and active proprietors, and John Locke, who became famous for the treatises he later wrote rationalizing the Glorious Revolution of 1688 in England. The weight of evidence suggests that Lord Ashley was the chief author and that Locke, as Ashley's secretary and as scribe for the proprietary group, advised, commented, and drafted policy statements at the request of the men in whom authority was vested and upon whom responsibility rested. [22]

A draft of the Fundamental Constitutions, dated 1669, was agreed to by the prospective colonists and presumably by the proprietors. However, the proprietors considered this draft incomplete, and in 1670 a finished document was sent to the colonials for endorsement. But their acceptance was never given.

This simple fact is the key that opens the door to a better understanding of the issues in dispute. The Charter of 1665 stated that the proprietors were authorized "to Ordain, make, and Enact, and under their Seals to Publish, any laws and Constitutions whatsoever, either appertaining to the Public State of the said whole Province or Territory, or of any distinct or particular County, Barony, or Colony of or within the same"; and now comes the essential qualification which is found in most colonial charters, "by and with the advice, assent, and approbation of the Freemen of the said Province or Territory, or of the Freemen of the County, Barony, or Colony For which such law or *Constitution* [my italics] shall be made, or the greater part of them, or of their Delegates or Deputies." [23]

Under these specifications, no system of government or

societal relationship could be imposed upon Carolina by the unilateral action of the proprietors. The semifeudal character of the Fundamental Constitutions complete with its prescriptions for distributing lands and titles, for an elaborate and somewhat contradictory judicial system, and for additional institutions to reinforce the highly structured interrelationships among the settlers—aspects of the document that have been the primary focus of scholars—had little if any relationship to the questions that troubled contemporaries. In effect, later generations of historians misrepresented the issue. They branded the Fundamental Constitutions as a fascinating but essentially amusing example of an archaic document, unworkable in the American setting and, therefore, to be discarded rather casually on the historical scrap heap as a quaint curiosity. Carolina contemporaries perceived the issue from a distinctly different point of view: any constitutional system unilaterally imposed was unacceptable. To them the issue was at once as simple and profound as self-government itself.

The reluctance of the freemen of Carolina to accept the Fundamental Constitutions can be readily understood in light of its language. It called for the establishment of a Carolina Parliament. This parliament was made up of the governor, the Grand Council composed of deputies of the proprietors, and elected delegates of the freemen sitting together in a single house to enact legislation. The Grand Council alone could propose bills; indeed, all measures were required to pass the Grand Council before they could be submitted to parliament. If the legislation was adopted, the Grand Council, now acting in an executive-judicial capacity, could veto parliamentary legislation. Within this political framework, elected freemen to the parliament, in relation to the decision-making and policy-making process, were scarcely more than ciphers.

That this provision in the Fundamental Constitutions

struck a sensitive issue is reflected in the exchange between the spokesmen for the proprietors and those of the petitioners, representing the colonials. "And the people haveinge *not* [my italics] accordinge to the Royall Charters assented or approved of any fundamentall Constitutions in Parliment [*sic*]," asserted the Carolina petition,

> have unanimously declared that the Goverment now is to be directed and mannaged wholy and solely accordinge to the said Charters,[;] and in particular the last Parliment did deny that any Bill must necessarily pass the Grand Councill before it be read in Parliment, and did profer [prefer] for the maintenance of peace and justice, to assent to & approve of any Law for that end, to be made accordinge to the directions and commands in the said Royal Charters . . .[;] but the Governor and the Lords Deputies pressinge to proceed as formerly, viz., by haveinge all Bills first past the Grand Councill, nothinge was don.[24]

In contrast, John Stewart, speaking for Governor Colleton, found the revisions for enacting legislation sought by the petitioners absurd. That "no bill shall pass but their way and in a new Channell" was a design to ensnare the governor. What motive could inspire such a demand "bot [but] malice or a designe of higher consequence than any yet dreams of." Unknowingly, Stewart's rhetoric catches a glimmer of reality.[25]

William Rivers, one of the earliest modern scholars to investigate the history of South Carolina, emphasizes that the "incomplete" version of the Fundamental Constitutions of 1669, at least so regarded by the proprietors, was altered in the 1670 version by the inclusion of a number of clauses, one of which encouraged the formation of an established Anglican church. This clause stated:

> As the Country comes to be sufficiently Planted and Distributed into fit Divisions, it shall belong to the Parliament to take care for the building of Churches and the public

> Maintenance of Divines, to be employed in the Exercise of
> Religion according to the Church of England, which, being
> the only true and Orthodox, and the National Religion of
> all the King's Dominions, is so also of Carolina, and there-
> fore, it alone shall be allowed to receive public Mainte-
> nance by Grant of Parliament.[26]

Rivers suggests that its inclusion prevented the Dissenters
from supporting the Fundamental Constitutions. He further hints that those who supported an established church
waited patiently for thirty years to fulfill their objective.

While the observation of Rivers sounds plausible, particularly in view of the contest that raged in the colony after
1700 to promote such an establishment, the evidence does
not support it. First, the Fundamental Constitutions confronted the colonials with a partial contradiction: a guarantee of religious toleration and participation in civil affairs
regardless of religious belief, and, at the same time, specific
instructions to establish the Anglican church. Second, the
protracted debate between 1670 and 1700 never focused
upon the particular clause referring to an established
church. Third, Anglicans as well as Dissenters vigorously
opposed the Fundamental Constitutions.

Even though the Fundamental Constitutions was eventually set aside, it operated de facto in selected areas of colonial affairs. During these years the South Carolina legislature was known as the "Parliament," a designation given
by the Fundamental Constitutions. For a time Parliament
operated much as it was designed to do, as a single body with
the Grand Council proposing legislation. Land was granted
under pertinent provisions of the Constitutions. In North
Carolina, Albemarle County was governed, for the most
part, according to the Fundamental Constitutions. In contrast to South Carolina, where the opposition to the Fundamental Constitutions was fierce, in North Carolina it never
emerged as a primary issue. As a result, the legislative ca-

pacity of North Carolina was crippled until well into the second decade of the eighteenth century, a phenomenon that will be subsequently explored.[27]

But in South Carolina the elected freemen were determined to separate themselves from a unicameral legislature dominated by the proprietary agents and to gain the right to initiate legislation. By 1692 the elected delegates were meeting separately in a Commons House of Assembly. They subscribed to their own rules of procedure; they elected a speaker of their own choice. They were not yet wholly free from the initiative of the Grand Council in proposing legislation, but they formulated bills for consideration. Members of the Commons House of Assembly used their parliamentary skill to exert pressure to modify legislation proposed by the Council, and at times they were able to delay or reject bills. During the 1690s the Commons House of Assembly definitely came into its own: initiating legislation, gaining control of the legislative process, and operating somewhat independently from the wishes of the proprietors.[28]

The Fundamental Constitutions, however modified by the proprietors to meet colonial critics, had been and remained a symbol: the imposition of a government by the proprietors without consultation or agreement with the colonists. The majority of colonials as represented by their elected delegates appealed to the Carolina Charters of 1663 and 1665 which stated in language that could not be misunderstood that laws were to be passed by and with their advice, assent, and approbation. The proprietors, on the other hand, argued that the charter gave them the right to make laws until such a time as the colony was sufficiently mature to be able to participate in the government, a position that could also be confirmed by a close reading of the charter. The proprietors contended that the Fundamental Constitutions was more generous than the charter in its guarantee of religious freedom and in its affirmation of political and civil rights. These arguments, in a technical, legalistic sense, may have been accurate, but they assumed acquiescence to a framework of government which the colonials had no part in forming and when accepted would seriously hamper any meaningful exercise of power.

Since the founding of the colony the colloquy on the Fundamental Constitutions had been ceaseless. As early as 1682, after a decade of agitation, more than half the representatives in the Carolina Parliament walked out of that body rather than sign the Fundamental Constitutions. Soon after Governor Colleton took office in 1686, a committee in the Carolina Parliament was appointed to inspect the Fundamental Constitutions and to propose alterations; but, in the language of contemporaries, "the worke grew volumious suddenly" and the committee's deliberations, in 1687, were "layd aside for some heates ariseinge in the howse." [29] When Governor Ludwell took office in 1691, the pendulum swung toward the point of view of the colonials, and in 1693 the proprietors acknowledged the position of the Carolina petitioners, in a proclamation dated 11 May 1693:

> And whereas the Inhabitants of our Province have desired rather to be governed by the full power granted to us by our Charter from the Crowne[—]as it was represented to us by Mr. Maurice Mathews he whom they did Impower to be their Agent[—]with which their desire Wee having complyed whereby the Rules and Limitations apointed by the sd. Constitutions for the Goverment [*sic*] are now ceased[;] and the Goverment of the said Province is to be for the future as it shall be directed by the Majority of Us the sd. Lords Proprietors of the sd. Province pursuant to the powers granted to us by our sd. Charter.[30]

As late as 1702 the proprietors tried to win the colonists to the position that the Fundamental Constitutions be accepted as a guide, but any effort made after 1693 was no more than a gesture. The proprietors and their spokesmen

entertained no expectation that the colonists would reverse themselves. Even in 1702 the question was only raised
because the Fundamental Constitutions guaranteed a remarkable degree of religious toleration; thus it was responsive to the most burning political-religious issue in the
colony at that time.

IV

No one would be so naive as to suggest that the men and
forces working to set aside the Fundamental Constitutions
and to bring about a larger measure of self-government were
free from the daily sweat of self-interest. A case in point was
that of representation in the Commons House of Assembly.
The proprietors in the 1680s, and again under Governor
Ludwell in the 1690s, sent instructions that the assembly of
South Carolina should be composed of seven delegates
from Colleton County, seven from Berkeley County, and six
from Craven. Berkeley County, of which Charleston was
the center, contained, according to an estimate made by
Ludwell, three-fourths of the population; yet it received
only one-third of the representation. The "frontier" counties of Colleton and Craven received representation far beyond what was justified on a democratic basis, an interesting
reverse of the usual generalization about the under-
representation of the frontier. Governor Ludwell suggested that the proprietors moderate the instruction with
regard to equal representation between the counties, but
the proprietors asserted that in the future the population
of Craven and Colleton would eventually catch up to that
of Berkeley. "Those that governe a Countrey that is Settling must have an Eye to the future, for Wee have reason
to hope that in time those Countys will come to have at least
each of them as many people as Berkley County and then

what right will it be that Craven County should choose but two and Berkly County 14."

Such statesmanlike foresight by the proprietors veiled a more immediate and powerful motivating force. In reality, they sought, by an equal allocation of delegates among the counties, to develop a proprietary party. By extending over-representation to Craven and Colleton counties, "Wee have reason to hope the French and all others will in time have their Eys opened and act more reasonably for our and their owne Interest." [31]

The instructions of the proprietors directly affected two principles involving representation: that a legislative body can determine for itself the establishment of election districts, a power which many, but not all, English colonies in North America exercised; and that representation should be in reasonable accordance with population, a principle little honored in colonial and United States history. In either case political power is the prize. With such high stakes in Carolina the leadership of Berkeley County resented the distribution of delegates among the counties, particularly as it applied to Craven whose population was not only sparse but composed almost exclusively of French Huguenots who had only recently arrived.

The Fundamental Constitutions protected these "aliens"; although the charter provisions were not explicit, the "Concessions of 1665" offered protection the equal of the Fundamental Constitutions. It is possible but unlikely that the decision of the Berkeley County leaders to oppose the Fundamental Constitutions was reinforced by a fear that their political influence would be undermined if the French received the protection of that constitutional framework. Berkeley County leaders with support from those of Colleton County had taken their stand on the Fundamental Constitutions well before the main body of Huguenots settled in Craven County. Furthermore, Berkeley County leaders took the initiative during Sothell's administration to adopt an act in 1691—negated by the proprietors in England along with the other enactments under Sothell—to confirm the civil and political rights of the French and Swiss Huguenots.[32]

The trinity of representation, self-government, and the Fundamental Constitutions was not the only development to awaken the tug of self-interest; also affected were the vital questions of land and Indian trade. In accordance with earlier agreements, the proprietors had set 1690 as the deadline to collect quitrents, payment to be made in specie. Contemporary complaints as found in Carolina letters and petitions expressed a distaste for making specie payments; payment in commodities produced in the colony was preferred. If this were the essence of the problem, it certainly would have been short-lived because the proprietors in their instructions to Governor Ludwell stated that they would be willing to accept commodity payment. Despite this concession, the dispute lingered. Carolinians were obviously reluctant to pay quitrents in any form. In addition, they, like all settlers in rapidly developing colonies, laid claim to more land than they were entitled to by patent; and they delayed taking the final steps toward full ownership in order to avert the payment of quitrents.

Grievances on land policy had plagued the colony from the beginning. In 1665, in a document entitled "Concessions and Agreements" made between the proprietors and the Barbadians who were being encouraged to settle in Carolina, the price of land had been set at one pence an acre. This agreement was not honored. In the 1680s and 1690s the terms governing land grants were less generous than those specified in the "Concessions." Complaints heard in other colonies were repeated in Carolina: the best land was allocated to the proprietors; the grants made to them were not only extensive but also contiguous, making settlement by an individual planter more difficult and settlement by a group of planters almost impossible; and friends of the proprietors received favored treatment at the expense of other settlers. A special fear persisted in Carolina that the proprietors would carve up the colony by permitting groups such as that of Lord Cardoss—who established a settlement of Scots at Port Royal and who asserted unequivocally that his "colony" had an independent political jurisdiction—to preempt the territory, denying opportunities for future land and profit to those already in the colony.

The procedure in granting land fell into a special category of grievances. The proprietors introduced a form of land conveyance, called an indenture, as a substitute for an outright deed, which required the grantee to sign a statement agreeing to begin payment of the appropriate quit-rent within six months or to forfeit the grant. No warrant to issue the grant or to survey it could be obtained until the prospective grantee signed this "reentry" clause. The prospect of laying out cash for a grant with a chance of losing it in six months was not attractive to Carolinians regardless of economic status.[33]

Whether the issue was representation, land policy, or some other question involving political content, the underlying proposition remained the same: so long as the Fundamental Constitutions remained the basis for governance, the proprietors determined policy because they controlled the pressure points of power. Eliminating the Fundamental Constitutions dramatically altered the character of the political contest.

In this context the issue of self-government is well represented in a list of grievances prepared in 1692–1693 by the delegates to the Commons House of Assembly: that the "office of Sheriffe and Judge of the Court of pleas" was "Lodged" in the same person, thereby uniting in a single man the prosecutor and judge; that though the creation of a court system was a proprietary prerogative, those courts "ought to be bounded and Regulated by Laws made by the assent of the people"; that public officers received fees in excess of those charged for similar responsibilities in England and these fees should "be settled by act of assembly here" in the same way that the Parliament in England determined fees; that too few people's delegates were in the Assembly, by which the colonists meant that the delegates representing the freeman could be out-voted by the governor and the proprietors' deputies in the Carolina Parliament; that the Palatine Court was working at cross purposes, invalidating legislation which the members of the court sitting as members of Parliament had "Ratified"; that the Palatine Court "putt in force" English laws that, in its judgment, were "addapted to this Province" without consulting the assembly; that the inferior courts in Carolina, whose membership was controlled by the proprietors through the governor, presumed to decide the extent of the powers of the Carolina House of Commons by determining the validity of their acts; and that the establishment of martial law, except in cases of rebellion, sedition, or invasion, exceeded the powers given by the proprietors under the charter. The recurring theme of this list reflects a fixed conviction on the part of the Carolina colonials that they, not the proprietors, must set policy.[34]

V

The conflict between the colonial demands to control policy and the prerogatives of the proprietors was resolved between 1694 and 1700 under the administrations of John Archdale (1694–1696) and his personally selected successor, Joseph Blake (1696–1700). The settlement did not extend to every detail of the complex interrelationship between proprietors and settlers, but it penetrated to the fundamentals: the distribution of land and payment of quitrents, but more significantly, the role of the Commons House of Assembly, representing the freemen, in establishing policy for South Carolina.

John Archdale came to Carolina at the request of his fellow proprietors, after Thomas Smith, a landgrave appointed temporary governor in 1693–1694, appealed to his superiors in England to send one of their number with authority to resolve the critical issues confronting the colony, especially those policies related to land; otherwise, Smith concluded with a flourish, the settlers would abandon the colony. The proprietors first asked Lord Ashley, grandson of the Earl of Shaftesbury, to undertake the task, but he declined, pleading a commitment to his father's business affairs. It is possible that he recognized a thankless task. Archdale, a Quaker who had purchased a proprietary share for his son in 1678, agreed to come.[35]

John Archdale was not a stranger to America, having worked unsuccessfully to develop the claim of Ferdinando Gorges in Maine. Upon returning to England he became a Quaker. His interest in North Carolina was aroused when a large number of Quakers had either settled there or been converted to the faith. Archdale is described as a person of moderate judicious temperament, an attribute in short supply. To judge from his writing, he was a man of learning, although he did not wear it lightly. Archdale visited North Carolina in 1683, and his return to the English colonies three decades after his first venture into the New World, this time to act on behalf of proprietors committed to a colony on the southern rather than the northern frontier, demonstrates once again the contagion of colonization; those engaged in it, however discouraging their earlier experience, never seemed to acquire immunity.[36]

Archdale writes that conflict interrupted the initial stages of his administration. "Some endeavour'd to sow Seed of Contention, thereby to nip the same; insomuch that they sat six Weeks under Civil Broils and Heats; but at length recollecting their Minds into a cooler Frame of Spirit, my Patience was a great means to overcome them; so that in the conclusion all Matters ended amicably." Although Archdale credited his own patience, the concessions he made to the colonials are more persuasive evidence.[37]

Archdale moved swiftly to resolve differences over land policy. Acting on instructions that he had solicited from the proprietors—although in certain details his colleagues in England complained that he exceeded instructions—the Governor instituted drastic changes in the distribution and sale of lands. These policies were incorporated in two acts: one, an Act to Ascertain Prices of Land, the Forms of Conveyances, Recovery of Rents, and Prices of Commodities for Payment; and two, an Act for Remission of Part of Arrears of Rent. Both were adopted 16 March 1696.[38]

Under the first act the price of land was greatly reduced, making it possible to purchase one thousand acres of land near the settled section of Carolina for twenty pounds current money; the same number of acres in the interior could be purchased for ten pounds. It was still necessary to pay a quitrent of twelve pence per one hundred acres, but, interestingly enough, failure to pay it did not prompt the immediate forfeiture of the land, thus evading the vexatious reentry clause, unless the lapse in payment extended to twenty-one years. This provision eliminated any immediate threat on the part of the proprietors to repossess land already granted. The law also provided that new settlers be exempted from quitrents for five years.

Adoption of the Act of Remission quieted but did not settle the land issue. From 1690, when quitrent payments were to begin, until 1694 when Archdale assumed office, collection lagged, even among affluent colonists. In an effort to enforce their will and to provide an object lesson, the proprietors instructed Governor Ludwell to initiate court proceedings against James Moore, a large landholder and leading Carolinian who was to become a member of the council and eventually governor.[39] This unsatisfactory state of affairs was eased only when Archdale and the assembly finally struck a bargain. The governor remitted quitrents for three years in some cases and four years in others. In response, the assembly adopted legislation requested by Archdale and needed by the colony: taxes to pay for the fortification of Charleston; procedures to expedite the payment of quitrents in the future; and a militia act, which included the provision that religious scruples could exempt a man from taking up arms.[40]

In the Commons House the effect of the quitrent remission was especially salutary. On the final day of the session, addressing the governor and the proprietors, the delegates singled out only one piece of legislation: "Wee . . . Profoundly Sencible of your Most Gratious Intimations Considerations and ffavours in . . . Investing . . . Archdale . . . with Such Large and ample powers . . . Doe Most Humbly Recognize and Sincerely and Cordially Thanke your Honours for the Late Acts of Grants Remission of Arrears of Rent The Undeniable Manifestation of your Honours Paternall Care of us Living in this your Collony." [41]

During his administration, Archdale made two concessions that illustrate how powerful the Commons House was becoming. First, the governor, when convening the session beginning January 1696, did not insist that Craven County be granted equal representation with Colleton and Berkeley. Berkeley and Craven jointly were allocated twenty delegates and Colleton ten delegates. When the Commons House met, the list of delegates did not contain a single French name, and no person who had represented Craven County in the two previous assemblies was elected. Berkeley County was able to exercise controlling influence, although the speaker selected was Jonathan Amory from Colleton. The concession made by Archdale on the allocation of delegates caused an uproar among his fellow proprietors in England. "Wee cannot aprove of your Expedient not to Grant Summons to Craven County to be represented in your Assembly as formerly." When Archdale explained that under the previous allocation of representatives, the number of eligible voters in Craven almost equalled the number of delegates—an overstatement of the case—the proprietors in England acquiesced.[42]

A second and equally significant concession to the Commons House is highlighted by the language of the Act to Ascertain Price and Conveyance of Land. Not only did its concluding clause declare that once the act was ratified by the governor and proprietors' deputies in Carolina it was not to be "repealed, annulled or revoked but by and with the consent of the Generall Assembly," but also that "this Act" was "unrepealable and irrevocable by any power or persons whatsoever, without the consent of the Generall Assembly."[43]

VI

Among the factors that enabled the colonials to take such a forceful stand was the growing weakness of the proprietors. Original proprietors such as Edward Hyde, the Earl of Clarendon and a minister during the reign of Charles II, and Anthony Ashley Cooper, the Earl of Shaftesbury, were giants in English politics during the Restoration period with its structured, contained society. During their primacy such men infused all governmental policy. Indeed, as late as the 1680s when the Crown attempted to regain control over all proprietary and charter colonies, the Carolina proprietors remained untouched.

But what a dramatic change had taken place by the late 1690s! Except for the Earl of Craven, the original proprietors were dead; Craven succumbed in 1697. In rare cases the proprietary legacy had been inherited by able sons and grandsons or assigned to competent guardians of minor children. But most titles changed hands when the proprietor died without heirs or when the proprietary right was sold. Generally the instructions in the 1690s were signed by only three of the following men: John Archdale, Thomas Amy, William Thornburgh, and the Earl of Craven. Although apparently fit, the earl was in his eighties; what energy he possessed was largely absorbed by domestic politics. Thornburgh acted as the guardian for the ten-year-old son of James Colleton, an arrangement that did not encourage a vigorous colonizing effort. Amy had been granted a proprietary share, apparently because he had helped to send colonists; his inexperience was never mitigated, so it would appear, by either talent or vision. However one might value his character, Archdale's claim of proprietorship was at best of doubtful legality, for Lady Berkeley, from whom he had reputedly purchased his share, had apparently sold the identical title to Amy. In the 1690s, therefore, the management of the colony of Carolina was in the hands of two men whose titles to a proprietorship were in doubt, a stand-in for a proprietor who was a minor, and a man whose age seriously limited his involvement. What is amazing is not that the colonials in the 1690s were able to gain ascendency in their struggle for power with the proprietors but that they did not overthrow proprietary rule altogether.[44]

A number of considerations delayed this ultimate step. First, the Crown, preoccupied with domestic and foreign problems resulting from the Glorious Revolution which placed William and Mary on the throne, did not encourage the Carolinians. To attempt to overthrow proprietary rule without at least the tacit consent of or assurance from the

Crown would have been foolhardy. Indeed, Carolinians did not express a desire to become a Crown colony at this time, no doubt recognizing that to gain control of the government of the colony only to relinquish it to the Crown was not in their best interest. When more was to be gained than lost by becoming a royal colony, this consideration was to be reappraised. Second, the seemingly limitless territorial boundaries of Carolina, extending from Virginia to present-day Florida and from the seaboard to the Mississippi River basin, deterred the consolidation of political strength. Finally, postponement of the eventual overthrow of the proprietors was an understandable corollary to a new and pre-eminent dimension in Carolina politics after 1700, the contest within the colony for control of policy.

The administration of Governor Joseph Blake, beginning in 1696 and ending with his death in 1700, was the longest of any early Carolina governor except for the second term of Joseph West, 1674–1682. The years of Blake's governorship can be classified as an era of good feeling, but as so often happens in such a period, those subterranean and contentious forces which were to dominate the following decade and to affect every Carolinian were already taking shape.

An important achievement during Blake's administration was "An Act for making Aliens free . . . and for granting Liberty of Conscience to all Protestants," adopted 10 March 1697. As early as 1693, after the foresighted act passed during Sothell's administration conferring the rights of English citizens on aliens in Carolina had been invalidated by the proprietors, the French Huguenots petitioned them to issue fresh instructions for a reenactment. The proprietors' reply could not conceal a pettiness of spirit. The French Huguenots, they declared, had been misled by men "who in the bottom love you not. . . . when you have tryed all you will find the Lords Proprietors themselves the best Friends you have." But, the proprietors concluded, "unwilling to take advantage of the Inconveniencys the said

Forraigners have contributed to bring on themselves by
joyneing with those who oposed the receiving the said Constitutions," they, the proprietors, agreed to instruct the governor to obtain legislation guaranteeing land titles and
conveyances.[45]

Under the terms of the act of 1697 aliens named in it or
those who petitioned the governor within three months
were granted rights the equivalent of those held by Englishmen, including the right to own, convey, and bequeath
property. Conveyances made previous to enactment of the
law were validated. A final clause in the act provided for
religious liberty—except for Catholics. Obviously, the
Huguenots gained the most from this legislation. The solution to the issue of the status of aliens, it should be noted,
was resolved not by proprietary order but on specific terms
formulated by the assembly.[46]

A fresh set of demands prepared by the Commons House
on 19 November 1698 reconfirms the consummation of a
decade of growing colonial political power and anticipates
the ultimate goal. The colony, the House asserted, should
have the right to coin money, a function considered the
prerogative of a sovereign; land grants must be confined to
one thousand acres, the unstated premise being that arbitrary awards by the proprietors were to be minimized; no
law could be enforced unless adopted by the colonial legislature; the governor and council, with the advice and consent of the assembly, should have the right to repeal any law
confirmed by the proprietors; the governor should be less
inhibited by his instructions. Including the governor and
council as a part of the demand for colonial political rights
reflects the realities of the political life, that Carolinians
possessed the power to control the governor—in fact if not
in theory.[47]

Having reached a new plateau, Carolinians could advance
to the next stage in their political education, an internal
struggle to control the policies of the colony.

TWO

Internal Politics
in Proprietary Carolina:
An Emerging Political Mosaic

IN THE 1690S THE POLITICS OF SOUTH CAROLINA WAS DOMIN-
ated by a struggle for power between the colonials and the
proprietors; during the decade after 1700 the struggle became a contest for control within the colony. The political
evolution of North Carolina, in contrast, cannot be cate-
gorized so neatly, one of numerous indicators that informs
the historian of the character of the mosaic subdividing the
southern colonies.

Before reviewing these developments, it is useful to re-
member that historians, by the nature of their profession,
describe, analyze, and explain events that have transpired.
They abhor conjecture as to what might have occurred. As
a result critical questions frequently are evaded.

In the case of Carolina, historians commonly assume that
the creation of two Carolinas, North and South, was somehow foreordained. It was not a presumption shared by the
proprietors. Because the separation of the Carolinas is taken
for granted, critical questions are seldom raised. For example, did the respective political experiences of the Albemarle and Ashley River settlements contribute to the ultimate division? And how is the historian to explain why the
political institutions of South Carolina, which in the 1690s

were based on counties as governing subdivisions, failed to develop the forms and functions of local government when these practices thrived in North Carolina?

I

Stripped to its essentials, the political struggle within South Carolina after 1700 involves a contest between counties, their interests and their constituencies, and the distribution of political power within a county which promoted or discouraged intercounty political alignments. Contemporary South Carolinians, it should be noted, frequently discussed rival political blocs within the framework of two principal religious groups, Anglicans and Dissenters. But these designations distort, if not falsify. Anglicans, considered as a religious affiliation, included a broad spectrum—high churchmen, moderate churchmen, and Englishmen with no genuine church allegiance but who out of custom associated themselves with the Anglican church. Dissenters, considered as a religious movement, included Presbyterians, Independents, and Quakers, depending upon their divergence from Anglican polity and doctrine. Many if not most Dissenters, however, had migrated from England. French Huguenots were, in fact, Dissenters, but they never classified themselves under this rubric.[1]

Not only do the terms "Anglican" and "Dissenter" fail to correspond with a precise religious affiliation, but they are also deceptive if used to designate political blocs. Stephen Bull, to cite an example, was an Anglican; but he was considered a member of the Dissenter bloc. The so-called Goose Creek Men, a half dozen prominent political leaders of Berkeley County, many of whom migrated from Barbados to take up lands along Goose Creek, a tributary of the Cooper River, were also Anglican. They opposed the "Dissenter coalition." [2]

Obviously, then, during this stress-filled period of South
Carolina politics no label accurately or fully reflects the
composition of political blocs. Only when the more general
terms, English-Anglican—which distinguishes between the
English and those French Huguenots who eventually became Anglican—and Dissenter, are correlated with an analysis of the population makeup and political influence within a county do patterns of political alignments emerge.[3]

The base of power for any political bloc within the colony
was the county, defined as a subdivision of the colony, not
as a unit of local government. Delegate strength in the Commons House of Assembly and the influence of these delegates upon legislative policy grew out of the informal personal and political associations of the constituency of the
county. Berkeley not only had the largest population of the
counties of South Carolina, but it was also the most hetero-
geneous, as could be expected of a county that included a
major port of entry, Charleston. The English-Anglicans ar-
riving from Barbados were probably the largest single segment of the population of Berkeley County, although a
specific figure cannot be cited with confidence. The population of Berkeley County also included a substantial number of Dissenters. At least three Dissenter churches flourished in Charleston compared with one Anglican church.
English-Anglicans and Dissenters resided in Charleston and
owned fertile land adjacent to the Cooper River and its
tributaries. French Huguenots, who as a group were generally not classified as Dissenters, comprised perhaps fifty
families in the population of Berkeley County.

In contrast to Berkeley, the population of Colleton and
Craven counties, located south and north of Charleston
respectively, were remarkably homogeneous. Colleton was
made up largely of Dissenters with a scattering of English-
Anglicans, but the Dissenters had such superiority in num-

bers that political control of the county was assured unless they divided over a grave political issue, a rare occurrence. Sparsely populated Craven County, located north of Berkeley and extending toward "North Carolina," was composed almost exclusively of French Huguenots.

The consequence of this population distribution within South Carolina dramatically illuminates the configuration of intracolonial political strife. Considered in terms of the entire population of South Carolina, the English-Anglicans and the Dissenters were nearly at a standoff. Arthur Hirsch, historian of the Huguenots of colonial South Carolina, suggests that on the basis of contemporary estimates the approximate ratio between Dissenter and Anglican populations was three thousand to twenty-five hundred. To accept such precision is treacherous. Even if correct, gross population figures cannot be equated with the number of persons who enjoyed the franchise. Regardless of the exact numbers, the base of Dissenter political power in Carolina was much more secure because of its grip upon Colleton County and thus its delegates to the Commons House, in contrast to the English-Anglicans who were never fully confident of controlling Berkeley County and its delegates to the Assembly. A modest number of defectors, joining with a bloc of Huguenots and Dissenters, could and did cause the Berkeley County English-Anglicans to lose their power base. And if one-fourth of the delegates of Berkeley County were Dissenters, that group allied with the Colleton delegation could determine Carolina policy. One indicator of the continuity of Dissenter strength is their domination of the office of governor which was held by Dissenters eighteen out of the first thirty years of the colony's existence. Craven County, inhabited by French Huguenots, was neither automatically in the political camp of the Dissenters nor in that of the English-Anglicans.[4]

II

Against this backdrop, two factors in the political contest emerge as being critical: first, the allocation of representation among the three counties; and second, the political allegiance of the Huguenots, who, despite their modest numbers, held the balance of power.

The apportionment of delegates to the Commons House between counties was altered radically between 1694 and 1696. Beginning in 1691 the allocation of representation in the Commons House was: Berkeley, seven; Colleton, seven; and Craven, six. In 1694 the governor and council, composed of Dissenters or men favorably disposed to them, wished to eliminate Craven County as a unit of representation, fearing that the Huguenots might align themselves with the English-Anglicans of Berkeley County. Ten delegates were allocated jointly to Craven and Berkeley and ten were allocated to Colleton. In August 1695 Governor John Archdale, recently arrived in South Carolina, issued writs for an election with an apportionment of delegates as follows: Berkeley, ten; Colleton, ten; Craven, none. But this decision was altered by the issuance of a writ for a new election in December, the governor summoning "all the Kings Leidge Subjects the freeman Inhabitants of Berkly and Craven Countys to bee and Appear" in Charleston. In reporting the results, Robert Gibbes, the sheriff, provided a list of twenty delegates for Berkeley and Craven jointly, with Colleton retaining only its original allocation of ten delegates. This pattern was followed in subsequent elections.[5]

What prompted these alterations in the apportionment for the Commons House is uncertain, but they obviously were related to the second factor in the intracolonial struggle for power, the political allegiance of the French Huguenots. A petition signed by a hundred inhabitants of Carolina, addressed to the governor and forwarded to the proprietors in August 1695, complained that instructions sent Governor Ludwell in 1691 resulted in the election of six Frenchmen from Craven as delegates to the Commons House, "which hath been very Dissatisfactory to the English here." The petition called for "an Assembly of Purely English and Elected onely by English." To call for an assembly with Frenchmen as delegates, they reported, "will be of Dangerous Consequence the English being highly incensed at it." [6] In August 1696 Governor Archdale observed: "the ffrench have never been told they Should not voat for or bee Elected members of Assembly but were for their owne Safeties and the preservacon of the publick peace perswaided to forbeare voting which if they had not Done at that time the ruining of this part of Your province had very probably followed." [7]

Contemporary comments quoted give the mistaken impression that opposition to the French Huguenots was supported by all political blocs; in reality the English-Anglicans were more favorably disposed to them than were the Dissenters, because they expected the political support of the French Huguenots. As early as 1690, when Governor James Colleton, a Dissenter, was replaced by Seth Sothell, the English-Anglicans not only led the opposition to Governor Colleton, but they were also given credit for passing enlightened legislation conferring the rights of British citizens upon French aliens, a measure originally vetoed by the proprietors. When Craven and Berkeley counties were coupled as a voting unit, the English-Anglicans were sensitive to the requirements of the Huguenots. Their ability to win political control of Berkeley and Craven counties depended on an alignment with the French.

The Dissenters, especially those residing in Colleton County, were aggressive in upholding British commercial regulations which specified that all trade must be carried on in vessels manned and owned by Englishmen. English-

Anglicans were willing to interpret imperial policies liberally, but Dissenters condemned ships and cargoes owned by the French Huguenots and profited personally from enforcement of the English Acts of Trade.[8]

Under the dispensation of ten delegates from Colleton and ten from Berkeley, the Dissenters, with their political base in Colleton secure, were at an advantage. The election of two or three Dissenters from Berkeley County gave them a slight political edge. Perhaps relying upon this strength, Dissenters during this period were amenable to concessions to English-Anglicans. However, moderation in the exercise of power was built in, because the Dissenters could not afford to alienate the Crown and Parliament.

When Archdale altered the allocation of representation between the counties in December 1695, giving Berkeley-Craven twenty delegates and Colleton ten, he set in motion three predictable developments which perhaps he did not foresee. First, the political advantage shifted slightly in favor of the English-Anglicans. Second, the French Huguenots became an even more critical voting bloc in Berkeley County, the stronghold of English-Anglican strength. And third, the Dissenters became increasingly, indeed, almost violently, anti-French.

The alteration in the political balance in favor of the English-Anglicans was confirmed in 1700 when James Moore became governor. He was the first English-Anglican to hold that office in more than a decade, gaining the post in a close contest. Only by a clever and successful maneuver was he able to block the selection of Joseph Morton, a Dissenter. The proprietors—albeit reluctantly in view of Moore's antiproprietary record—confirmed James Moore's appointment.[9]

Because of the narrow margin of victory, it might be expected that Moore and the English-Anglicans would opt for compromise. Instead, they sought to enlarge their advantage by unexpectedly forceful measures. They acted to give the Huguenots the franchise—because they were supporters—without extending the privilege of officeholding. To consolidate their political control, within five years the English-Anglicans were prepared to take the extraordinary step of excluding Dissenters from office.

In 1700 Governor Moore issued writs for an election calling for ten delegates from Colleton County and twenty from Berkeley-Craven. If the number of votes cast is used as the criterion in the apportionment of delegates, to the disadvantage of Colleton, then Moore's call appears to be justified. But the governor's critics complained that he compromised the election by bringing in unqualified voters. "Much threat'nings, many intreaties & other unjustifiable actions were made use of, & illegal and unqualify'd votes given in to the Sheriff, & by him receiv'd & returned," asserted the petitioners,

> particularly the votes of very many unqualify'd Aliens were taken & enter'd, the votes of several Members of the Council were fil'd & receiv'd, a great number of Servants & poor & indigent persons voted promiscuously with their Masters & Creditors, as also several free Negroes were receiv'd, & taken for as good Electors as the best Freeholders in the Province. So that we leave it with Your Lordships to judge, whether admitting Aliens, Strangers, Servants, Negroes, &c, as good and qualified Voters, can be thought any ways agreeable to King *Charles'* Patent to Your Lordships, or the *English* Constitution of Government.[10]

Out of seven new delegates in Berkeley County, two, John Crosskeys and Robert Fenwick, were outright Dissenters, and one, Stephen Bull, was a moderate churchman who received Dissenter support and was properly considered a member of their political bloc. At the same time warm friends of the church such as James Risbee and Charles Burnham were turned out of office. The results, then, represented a modest rather than dramatic shift in the composition of the Commons House, but it was sufficient to place the English-Anglicans of Berkeley County in positions of leadership.[11]

Governor Moore used his newly won gains to obtain the reluctant approval of the Commons House to mount an expedition to attack the Spanish at St. Augustine, Florida, but the expedition itself turned into a military and financial disaster. As a consequence the colony incurred four thousand pounds sterling of debt, which was quickly transformed into a political issue. Attempts to regulate the Indian trade also failed in the Commons House.[12]

Never a patient man and certainly not a bashful one, the governor campaigned to broaden his political support in the Commons House, and a new call for elections was issued. The voter turnout in Berkeley County was spectacular. In previous elections a vote of 150–200 gave a candidate a comfortable victory margin, but in this case the big winners backed by Moore almost doubled the number of voters. Moore's opponents cried fraud, and a new call for elections was issued. "We further represent to Your Lordships," they petitioned the proprietors,

> that contrary to the rights & priviledges which we ought to enjoy, the last Election of Members to serve for *Berkly* County was managed with greater injustice to the Freeman of this Province than the former. For at this last Election, Jews, Strangers, Sailors, Servants, Negroes, & almost every *French* Man in *Craven* & *Berkly* County came down to elect, & their Votes were taken, & the Persons by them voted for were returned by the Sheriff, to the manifest wrong & prejudice of other Candidates.[13]

Popular Dissenters such as John Crosskeys and Robert Fenwick failed reelection. When the members of the Commons House were sworn, all except a half-dozen accepted the Oath of Supremacy, an indication of the growing

English-Anglican strength. Petitions were promptly submitted to the Commons House contesting the returns. Numerous voters were summoned to the House where their
right to vote was challenged. This review induced a legislative paralysis; the hearings, in themselves, demonstrated
that, regardless of the election and its results, the Commons House did not act either as the servant of the governor
or as an arbitrary authority. Despite its pronounced English-
Anglican constituency, the Commons House conducted itself as a self-governing institution, with full recognition of
appropriate legislative procedures.[14]

The review conducted by the Commons House failed to
satisfy the Dissenters of Colleton County. They recognized
that a minimum of five Dissenters needed to be elected to
the Berkeley delegation of twenty if the Dissenters were to
regain control of the Commons House. With an English-
Anglican as governor, this objective became more urgent.
Therefore, Dissenters began increasingly to concentrate on
the alignment between the French Huguenots and the
English-Anglicans, with the elimination of the political
power of the Huguenots as their goal.

III

In June 1703 the Dissenters prepared and signed a petition
of grievances addressed to the proprietors. In it they denied
that the issue was merely a temporary reduction of their
political strength; instead, they claimed a breach of their
fundamental rights.

> But considering that the very Foundation of our lawful
> rights, hath of late been struck at by Persons, who have
> more regard to their private Interest than the publick good,
> we humbly conceive, that it cannot stand with the Duty we
> owe to our selves as *Englishmen*, or to our Posterity, to sit
> down contented with less than that which every Liege and

Freeborn Subject of the Crown of *England* may, and of right ought to have. And, therefore, lest our silence should be prejudicial to so important a cause, we humbly crave Your Lordships leave, faithfully and impartially to represent to you the great and notorious violations & infringements of our Laws and Liberties, under which we suffer.[15]

"Are we to be ruled by foreigners?" asked the Colleton Dissenters. "For when once our lawful Rights & privileges are denied us, when Foreigners & Strangers shall make our laws" then resident English suffer the loss of their liberties. Indeed, "no Alien born out of the Allegiance of the Crown of *England*, unless he be otherwise especially qualifyed, ought to elect for, or be elected to serve as a Member of Assembly." The Dissenters denounced the alleged machinations of the English-Anglicans of Berkeley County. "As to the *French*, they have hitherto lived peaceably, & with due encouragement amongst us; but when we see & consider that they are often made tools of & imposed upon, & persuaded by ill-designing Persons here, to carry on sinister Designs, to the general disadvantage of the Country . . . we can't imagine that we do them any hurt, by making good and wholesome Laws for us & them." [16]

The petition also included a predictable but largely unsubstantiated indictment against Governor Moore—his self-interest in the Indian trade, his attack on St. Augustine reputedly to divert the Commons House from other issues, and his falsification of election returns. The only complaint for which evidence exists is the possible influence of Moore and his supporters at the polls and the physical threats to the Dissenters by such English-Anglican extremists as Captain George Dearsley and Captain William Rhett. Even this charge must be treated with caution. In reviewing the Commons House list of delegates, for example, Dearsley was a member of the assembly of 1698 under Blake, a Dissenter, and Rhett cooperated with the Blake. Neither Dearsley nor Rhett was elected a member of the House when the English-Anglican group supporting Moore made modest gains in the membership of that chamber in 1700.[17]

By the time the petition of the Colleton County Dissenters was signed on 26 June 1703, Nathaniel Johnson, a determined Anglican churchman and former governor of the Leeward Islands who had lived in Carolina since the political troubles of 1690, had been officially appointed governor of Carolina by the proprietors. When the petition was written, it was, in many respects, already dated. Certainly, when John Ash, a Colleton County leader, described by former Governor Archdale as "not a Person suitably qualified to Represent their State here [in England], not that he wanted Wit but Temper," presented the petition in England, its force was spent.[18]

Originally drawn up to attack a modest target—the controversial election returns in 1700, 1701, and 1702—the petition, in an odd, almost inadvertent way, was eventually employed to counter a genuine threat, an attempt to curtail the political rights of Dissenters by divesting them of the privilege of officeholding, an action taken a year after the petition was drawn up. To achieve this end, the extremists among the English-Anglicans used the vehicle of an established church. Considered in the long term, the church establishment was most influential in developing the social-religious institutions which were to operate in the colony for three-quarters of a century. In the short term, however, the significance of the issue was its explosive political content: How would the formation of an established church affect the balance of power in the internal politics of Carolina?

The issue, as it developed, was indigenous to Carolina. It did not arise or take form at the initiative of the proprietors. Only as the issue became increasingly heated was it projected into the proprietary deliberations, and ultimately to the Crown.

This assertion is not to suggest that the events in Carolina took place in isolation. Indeed, shortly after 1700 England attempted to adjudicate the question of the political rights of Dissenters, and Parliament engaged in a passionate debate on the issue. No doubt news concerning these events in England encouraged Governor Johnson to take the bold step of disbarring the Dissenters from the franchise. But the distribution of delegate strength in the counties and the composition of political blocs had already determined the dimensions of the issue in South Carolina.

Adopted in May 1704, "An Act for the More Effectual Preservation of the Government of This Province, By Requiring All Persons That Shall Hereafter be Choosen Members of the Commons House of Assembly . . . To Conforme to the Religious Worship in this Province According to the Church of England," excluded, in effect, the Dissenters from membership in the Commons House of Assembly. It was enacted by a majority of one vote. "As nothing is more contrary to the profession of the Christian Religion, and particularly to the doctrine of the Church of England, than persecution for conscience only" the preamble declared,

> nevertheless, whereas it hath been found by experience that the admitting of persons of different persuasions and interest in matters of religion to sitt and vote in the Commons House of Assembly, hath often caused great contentions and animosities in this Province, and hath very much obstructed the publick business; and whereas by the laws and usage of England, all members of Parliament are obliged to conforme to the Church of England, by receiving the sacrament of the Lord's Supper accornidg [*sic*] to the rites of the said church; *Be it, therefore enacted.*[19]

The vote on the so-called Exclusion Act does not reveal the precise numerical division between the English-Anglicans and the Dissenters in the Commons House. In every assembly after 1700 the substantial majority of delegates, often as many as two-thirds, took the prescribed Anglican Oath of Supremacy instead of exercising the right of mere affirmation. Because the contemporary material relating to the vote on the Exclusion Act is either fragmentary or a part of a "Case for the Dissenters," a final judgment is precluded, but the indication is that a sufficient number of English-Anglicans in the Commons House found the disbarment of Dissenters so high-handed as to constitute a permanent threat to acceptable governmental institutions and political behavior.

On 4 November 1704, about six months after the Exclusion Act, the Commons House passed and the governor hastily signed an act to establish the Anglican church. It set out the appropriate arrangements for an established church: parishes were designated, in some cases complete with boundaries; tax payments to support the church were fixed; authority to impress laborers to build the parish churches and complementary buildings was granted; authority to impress slaves in respective parishes to work was specified; and clergymen were to be selected by a majority of the inhabitants of the parish.

The sacrament of marriage was to follow the Table of Marriage as provided by the Church of England, placing in question ceremonies performed by Dissenting clergy. The responsibilities and conduct of vestries were defined. An extraordinary section of the act established a supervising group of twenty laymen called commissioners. The first commissioners were listed in the act and included the leading figures of the English-Anglican party: Governor Johnson, former Governor James Moore, and Job Howes, a member of the Commons House frequently elected to the speakership. Proposing a body of commissioners was an ingenious attempt by the English-Anglicans in Carolina to achieve multiple objectives, eliminate Dissenters from politics and at the same time minimize the influence of the church establishment. Nothing was to be left to chance. The commissioners were authorized to review the conduct of the clergy, which included the power to rescind an appointment to a particular parish. The act exceeded seven thousand words in length, unmistakable evidence that it was long in preparation.[20]

A second act adopted the same day, entitled "An Act to Regulate the Elections of the Members of the Assembly," was brief put potent. It granted the franchise to persons over twenty-one years of age who were resident in the county and who owned fifty acres of land or ten pounds value in goods, rents, or chattels. An Act for Making Aliens Free granted "aliens" the rights of British citizens in every regard, including the franchise, but it did not permit them to serve as members of the Commons House of Assembly. This qualification followed the lead of Parliament which forbade political officeholding by aliens.[21]

According to contemporary accounts, the Establishment Act of November 1704 as well as the early Exclusion Act of May 1704 was accepted by the proprietors on a divided vote —Archdale, the former governor and Quaker, and Maurice Ashley being opposed. The Earl of Granville, a confirmed and forceful Church of England man and now the most prestigious proprietor, championed both acts, and, reputedly, to validate them, he cast his vote and the two votes he held in proxy in the affirmative. Whether these accounts were accurate is uncertain.[22]

What is certain is that Joseph Boone headed a group of petitioners, composed principally of London merchants trading with Carolina, to present the House of Lords with a list of their grievances. What had been said about the elections between 1700 and 1702 was now repeated about the election of 1703. "The election was managed with very great partiality and injustice, and all sorts of people, even Servants, Negroes, Aliens, Jews, & Common Sailors, were admitted to vote in Elections." The petition to the House of Lords condemned that part of the Establishment Act which was the most vulnerable, the "Ecclesiastical Commission" in the colony which had already taken action against Edward Marston, the Anglican clergyman in Charleston, who was regarded by the governor and his friends as "a pest." The act calling for conformity was condemned as "illegal" because the Commons House met in April 1704 and adopted the act on May 6 when, according to the petitioners, the House was, as slated in the original writ, supposed to be in adjournment.[23]

Outside Parliament, the Dissenters enlisted the pen of Daniel Defoe, who wrote a pamphlet, *Party-Tyranny*, published in 1705. The pamphlet includes a predictable compilation of documents, but it is preceded by an arresting constitutional argument. The Carolina Exclusion Act, Defoe contended, was tyrannical and invaded English liberty. Defoe then raised the question of the authority of Parliament and the relationship of colonial peoples regarding that authority:[24]

If any Man shall say this Matter is not Cognizable in Parliament, and that the People of Carolina are not represented here, having a Parliament of their own, by whom they are to be Determin'd, that they are therein entirely under the Government of themselves, and that these Oppressions are the Act and Deed of their own Representative, and therefore their own Act and Deed, I shall take leave to Answer.

Tis true, by the Constitution of Carolina, they are under the Government of themselves, and perhaps if their Constitution were rightly Administred, it may be allow'd the best Settlement in America. But as the Wisdom of their Constitution is known, and unquestion'd, without doubt those able Heads that settl'd their Government, did not forget, that even those Representative Assemblies, especially in the Infancy of the Government, might be corrupt, or might by Bribery or other ill Practices, be Modell'd and Influenc'd in Matters of Parties, to Oppress and Injure the people they acted for. . . .

That when any Body of Men Representative, or other Acting by, or for a Constitution, from whom they receive their Power, shall Act, or do, or make Laws and Statutes, to do anything destructive of the Constitution they Act from, that Power is *Ipso facto* dissolv'd, and revolves of Course into the Original Power, from whence it was deriv'd.

Then Defoe turned to a discussion of the source of power which in part reinforced English authority but which in part contradicted the reality of self-government as it was being developed in the English colonies in America:

From hence it must follow, that upon known Depredations of Common Liberty, Breach of the Capitulations of Government, between the Governors and the People of Carolina; the People without doubt, by Right of Nature as well as by the Constitution, revolves under the immediate Direction and Government of the English Empire, whose Subjects they were before, and from whom their Government was deriv'd. . . .

In England the House of Lords agreed to hear Boone's petitions. After exploring the consequences of the South Carolina Exclusion Act, the Lords resolved on 9 March 1706 that the Carolina legislation violated the laws of England. A few days later that prestigious body sent an address to the Queen asking that the Crown act to relieve the Carolina colonials from this arbitrary oppression. The Queen then directed the proprietors to disallow the Exclusion Act.[25]

Learning of the action taken by the House of Lords, Governor Johnson anticipated the disposition of the Crown by recommending to the Commons House of Assembly of South Carolina that it repeal the Exclusion and the Establishment Acts of 1704. In his request the governor recognized the opposition of the Society for the Propagation of the Gospel in Foreign Parts to that part of the act which granted the Carolina commissioners almost exclusive authority over the church. Indeed, the society had refused to send ministers until the power of the commissioners was rescinded or at least modified. The Commons House acted promptly upon the governor's recommendations.[26]

The governor further recommended the adoption of a new Church Establishment Act which produced the Church Act of 1706, more moderate in tone and in consequence than that of 1704. Ten parishes were created; Berkeley was divided into six parishes, Craven one, with the remaining three assigned to Colleton. Glebes were authorized for the clergy, and annual salaries were specified. Inhabitants of the parish retained the power to select their ministers, a congregational aspect of Church of England polity in America that ran parallel to the experience of Virginia. Commissioners for Carolina were established, but with restricted authority as compared with the act of 1704. Seven vestrymen for each parish selected by their fellow churchmen were to carry out duties as authorized in the act. Expenses not covered by gifts or by the other fees were to be paid by means of an assessment upon each and all inhabitants of the parish. In short, a comprehensive church establishment was formulated, to be refined further by an act adopted in 1708.[27]

Repealing the offensive conformity act and moderating the church establishment did not appear to produce a radical turnabout in political affairs. It certainly did not mark a great advance on the part of one social group or the fulfillment of a social revolution, because Dissenters were equal in wealth and status to English-Anglicans. The French churches were gradually assimilated into the established

Anglican church; the French offered political leadership as well as votes. The anti-French position of the Dissenters moderated as a political balance was restored.

The makeup of the Commons House delegations of Berkeley and Colleton counties changed slightly, but, surprisingly, the membership immediately succeeding the repeal of the Exclusion Act accepted without question or debate the Oath of Supremacy. Not a single member chose mere affirmation, a practice commonly exercised before the Exclusion Act. This result underscores the conclusion that a political balance rather than religious convictions was at the root of the internal political conflict in South Carolina.

IV

Sheared of extremism, the English-Anglican and Dissenter political blocs turned to two pressing problems that had been persistently projected into the intracolonial struggle for power after 1700 and the politics of the establishment issue: (1) the rivalry with the Spanish—to a much more limited degree the French—which occasionally exploded into a military confrontation, and (2) the regulation of the Indian trade.

Between 1700 and 1702 policy decisions made with respect to Spanish Florida aroused furious opposition from a small minority of the Commons House. John Ash, the leading petitioner among the Dissenters, revealed an absence of restraint that insulted reason as he asserted that Governor Moore was planning to undertake this expensive expedition solely for private plunder. When the expedition failed and the colony found itself with a debt of four thousand pounds, Moore and others suggested that bills of credit be issued, a practice accepted in Massachusetts and later followed by most English colonies from Massachusetts to Carolina. Ash attempted to use this request to gain a political trade-off:

issuance of bills of credit in return for passage of two measures formulated by him; an election law, the terms of which are unknown but probably directed against the French; and an act to regulate the Indian trade. Moore succeeded in getting his bills of credit, but Ash failed to get his election law and regulatory legislation. Ash's frustration affected his subsequent actions, including his decision to leave the Commons House in the spring of 1703 and to prepare the Colleton Dissenter Petition of June 1703—a year before the Exclusion Act and eighteen months before the Church Establishment Act. Obviously, provocative political manipulation was not confined to the English-Anglicans.[28]

The reality of the Spanish rivalry was dramatized in August 1706 when five French privateers, reinforced by Spanish troops, disembarked near Charleston. Their appearance threw the population into a temporary fright, but the threat to Charleston was dissipated when a united colony faced the intruders, defeated them, and ended, at least for a time, the fear that Spanish or French forces would reappear momentarily at the wharves of Charleston. In retrospect, these eruptions between Spanish Florida, France, and Carolina represent incidents in the struggle between the European nations to achieve a world balance of power, a subject of singular importance but one that has no place in this discussion. In terms of the immediate political setting, however, the Carolina adventure to St. Augustine in 1702 exacerbated internal political conflict within South Carolina rather than caused it. A successful expedition against Spanish Florida in 1704 relieved the tension but did not end it.[29]

As a corollary of international rivalry, the issue of the Indian trade was never wholly absent from the political debate between 1700 and 1710, but specific action was not taken until 1707. The issue was complicated by four simultaneous developments: the growing international rivalry among England, France, and Spain for shares in the Indian trade;

Carolina's challenge of Virginia's ties to the Indian nations occupying the territory of the southern Applachians; the proprietors' demand for exclusive trading rights; and, last, by the intracolonial struggle between the principal Carolina leaders and the multitude of small traders. Indian enslavement and exploitation, reprehensible conduct by individual Indian traders, or other policies or practices at one level of rivalry reverberated at all levels. When the Indians were encouraged to make war against each other or against European settlers, the trade in deerskins inevitably declined abruptly. Warriors have no time to hunt; no skins or fur, no trade or profit.

As the fulcrum of political power in Carolina changed, control over the Indian trade changed. At the outset of settlement the proprietors managed the Indian trade. As their power weakened in the 1680s and became enfeebled in the 1690s, Carolina colonials took control over this profitable enterprise. But they quarreled among themselves over who should be permitted to engage in it and who should be excluded.

Except for an abortive act adopted during the administration of Governor Sothell, no statute on Indian trade was enacted during the 1690s, but the record reveals unmistakably that the Commons House presumed it possessed the power to initiate regulatory legislation. In 1698, for example, the Commons House, acting as a committee of the whole, debated a bill to regulate the Indian trade. What should be included in the bill was reviewed: the issuance of public stock, the concept that every man could act as a free trader on his own plantation, and the appointment of commissioners to enforce regulations. Although the bill was finally rejected, a message from Governor Joseph Blake to the House clarifies the dominant role of the Commons House in the management of the Indian trade: "And if you have thoughts of an adjournment we Desire you will not Expect it for to Long time And that you will before you rise this meeting, (Since you have not approved of your owne Bill Lately before you for Regulateing the Indjan Trade) Appoynt a Committee to Consider of Some other way of Regulateing it [the Indian trade] against your next Sitting."[30]

In effect, the failure to act in 1698 preserved the status quo. Theoretically, the trade was open to everyone; but because of the capital required to bring in trading goods as well as the experience and connections within Indian country that were necessary prerequisites to produce results, the trade, in fact, was best utilized by the principal men of Carolina, Dissenters as well as English-Anglicans. After 1700 Ash and the Colleton Dissenters tried to make the issue a partisan one by accusing Governor Moore of attempting to monopolize the trade, but the evidence contradicts them. Moore offered several options for a licensed, open trade regulated by the Commons House by means of commissioners. When an enactment was finally agreed upon, the Commons House appealed to Moore's proposal as the precedent for their act.

The controversy over control of the Indian trade persisted during the bitter embroilment of the Exclusion Act and Church Act. During the winter session of the Assembly in 1706–1707 when Governor Nathaniel Johnson called for repeal of both disruptive enactments, he urged, in an extraordinary personal way, that an act to regulate Indian trade be adopted: "Once more I offerr you a Regulac'on of the Indian Trade but so that it may be safe to the Countrey[,] Honourable and proffitable to my self[,] and no way Chargeable to the publick." His candid comment concluded a series of exchanges during the session between the Governor and the Commons House over the regulation of the trade. The Commons House responded in an address signed by Speaker William Rhett, an outspoken English-Anglican, that the terms proposed by the House were reasonable.[31]

An act to regulate the Indian trade was finally adopted on

19 July 1707. Support for it came from all political blocs. Thomas Nairne, a leading figure from Colleton County, and Richard Beresford, an unimpeachable English-Anglican, represent the quality and experience of the advocates. When Governor Johnson experimented with a final delaying tactic, the House responded that it was unwilling to vote for fortifications unless the governor consented to an act of regulation: "We are not Sollicitous to provide a defence for Our breasts when we may at the Same Time receiue a mortall Stabb: thro Our Backs." [32]

The act called for the licensing of traders and carried penalties for selling liquor and ammunition to the Indians or for taking goods from them by force or by inducing conditions that implied force. Thomas Nairne was appointed the resident Indian agent. Ralph Izard, James Cochran, Richard Beresford, John Ash, John Abraham Motte, and John Fenwick were appointed commissioners, a relatively balanced contingent of Dissenters, English-Anglicans, and Huguenots. Under the terms of the act the commissioners were to prepare the regulations for the everyday conduct of the trade and to serve as a court to adjudicate infractions. Adjustments to the act itself were made frequently in subsequent years, and regulations by the commissioners were modified almost every year to accommodate changing conditions. Regardless of the adjustments, the act was never wholly satisfactory. As early as 1711 it was asserted that none of the traders in the Indian country took the trouble to acquire a license. The question of Indian trade and Indian relations was obviously in its opening rather than its concluding phase.[33]

In return for accepting the act of 1707, Governor Johnson demanded and received an outright gift of four hundred pounds in lieu of the annual revenue that he customarily received in Indian presents. Johnson and succeeding governors were also to receive as additional compensation one hundred pounds annually.[34]

The appointment of the public receiver for South Carolina was briefly ensnarled in the debate over the Act on Indian Trade. Governor Johnson considered this appointment a pawn to obtain a larger stipend from the Commons House for relinquishing the prerogative of receiving presents from the Indians. He claimed that he had the right to nominate the receiver, even though, in fact, the Commons House had exercised this authority for a decade. The governor abandoned this position when he received the grant of four hundred pounds from the Commons House.

In December 1708 Edward Tynte was appointed governor to replace Nathaniel Johnson, but Tynte died soon after taking office. He was succeeded by Charles Craven. By the time Governor Johnson left office, however, the political pattern, as it operated until the overthrow of the proprietary government, was established. The South Carolina colonials had gained firm control of their own destiny. After 1700 the internal struggle for power, after a spasm of dramatic confrontation by extreme factionalism, resulted ultimately in a relatively stable and balanced political alignment.

V

Fragmentary evidence denies the scholar the opportunity to provide the same detailed analysis of the politics of North Carolina from 1690 to 1715 as that of South Carolina, but the dissimilarity in their political evolution reinforces the mosaic character of the southern colonies at an early date. Although contemporaries agree that the Quakers controlled the Assembly of North Carolina after 1690—and probably before that date—the records cannot be checked for confirmation because they do not exist in any consistent form. In most cases, therefore, isolated bits of correspondence and other evidence from one group of partisans must be evaluated against that of another. In either case, conclusions must be hedged with qualifications. The absence of documentary material is reflective of the character of early North Carolina, a colony sparsely settled with a scattered population and unformed political institutions given to an episodic history. There is not the faintest indication that North Carolina would become the fourth most populous English colony in North America by the time of the American Revolution.

Although North and South Carolina attained the same objective, the eventual overthrow of proprietary rule, the route taken to achieve it reflected their respective strengths and weaknesses. In the 1690s South Carolina gained political maturity by its confrontation with the proprietors. Assured of an ascendant position in relation to the proprietors, South Carolina then faced the issues of an internal contest for positions of authority and power in which the political content of the Exclusion Act and Church Act of 1704 figured significantly, but at no time after 1690 or 1700 were the institutions of self-government in South Carolina in jeopardy. The struggle in South Carolina took place within a political framework accepted by the forces in contention for power.

In contrast, the political institutions of North Carolina were neither well developed nor accepted by contesting political groups. In particular, the establishment of the Fundamental Constitutions as the basis of government in Albemarle emasculated the power exercised by the assembly and enhanced that of the council, whose members were directly appointed by the proprietors and who spoke for them. The result was the enfeeblement of popular political institutions and processes. The North Carolina colonials could not and did not stand up to the power of the proprietors. Political settlements arrived at internally were always tentative. The slightest pressure from the proprietors or the most trivial internal problem tended to produce political tremors that often degenerated into monumental chaos. The political assurance, the concept of an accepted framework of political institutions, the assumption that decisions reached within the colony would stand regardless of external forces, so characteristic of the political evolution of South Carolina between 1690 and 1710, were absent in North Carolina. If the political groups of South Carolina were fractionated, those of North Carolina were atomized. If the political alignments of South Carolina changed but remained identifiable, those of North Carolina were so splintered as to verge on the edge of anarchy.[35]

These characteristics colored the political life of early North Carolina and it followed a distinctive course. The overriding consideration in South Carolina politics during the 1690s was to reduce the power of the proprietors, but this issue was not raised in North Carolina for two decades. North Carolina was still in the process of establishing a dependable set of political institutions. As late as 1713 Lieutenant Governor Spotswood of Virginia, irritated by events in Albemarle, wrote: "There reigns such stupidity and Dissention in the Government of North Carolina that it can neither concert any measures nor perform any engagements for its own Security." [36]

Those political institutions available to North Carolina in the 1690s were fragile weapons with which to confront the proprietors. At the same time, undependable political organization and institutions encouraged a pronounced individualism. A contemporary critic unintentionally paid the Albemarle colonials a tribute when he intimated that they were a lawless people allowing no power or authority in either church or state except that which was derived from them. The countervailing forces of heightened individualism versus proprietary dominance, not merely for the 1690s but for the early eighteenth century, increased political tension which, in turn, triggered sweeping, abrupt, and sometimes violent political upheavals.

When Philip Ludwell was made governor of the Carolinas in 1691, he appointed Thomas Jarvis, a North Carolinian, to serve as his deputy there. Ludwell had been instructed by the proprietors to call an assembly representing North Carolina and South Carolina to meet in Charleston, but the instruction was impossible to implement. The allocation of representatives designated in the instruction, three for South Carolina to one for North Carolina, is a reliable, if somewhat exaggerated, assessment of how contemporaries rated the relative strength and potential of the two areas of settlement.

An incident surrounding the appointment of Ludwell as governor reflects the temper of the times. John Gibbs claimed that when Seth Sothell was removed from the government of North Carolina, he, Gibbs, had been elected governor by the council. In a declaration issued 2 June 1690, he denounced Ludwell as "a Rascal, imposter, and Usurper." He sent out a call to "keep the King's peace" and "to consult the ffundamentals," meaning, of course, the Fundamental Constitutions; and he urged the populace to give him their allegiance. If a Ludwell supporter decided to take to the sword, Gibbs remarked, "I will single out and goe with him into any part of the King's Dominions, and there fight him in this Cause, as long as my Eyelids shall wagg." Gibbs, like self-styled insurrectionists who preceded and followed him, eventually fled to Virginia.[37]

The arrangement of a deputy governor appointed by the resident governor in South Carolina was followed until 1710, when Edward Hyde received an appointment directly from the proprietors to become governor of North Carolina. This action is usually interpreted by historians as an acknowledgment by the proprietors that Albemarle settlements were to become a separate colony. The evidence to support this view is not only insubstantial but unclear. Certainly, there was no break in the political process of the colony.[38]

So far as the evidence is available, good will seems to have prevailed in the relationship between the proprietors and the settlers during the 1690s. Preoccupied with the unrest and discontent in South Carolina, the proprietors virtually ignored North Carolina. Governor Archdale's appointment in 1694 was welcomed. He had visited the colony a decade earlier; he was a Quaker, and the Quakers in North Carolina held many of the principal executive and judicial offices and exercised leadership in the assembly. Stephen B. Weeks, the historian of Quakerism in North Carolina, asserts that the period between 1675 and 1700 was its golden age.

Between 1700 and 1715 the politics of North Carolina took a turn that more closely paralleled the experience of South Carolina: factions contesting for political control. The principal issue, as in South Carolina, was the creation of an Anglican church establishment; but much more was involved than a difference of religious views. The issue awakened renewed political rivalry between the antiestablishment group led by the Quakers and the establishment group led by those loyal to the Church of England. In contrast to South Carolina, the proprietors played a significant role in this struggle, but their precise influence cannot be accurately gauged. After 1715 when an acceptable political compromise was reached, North Carolina finally exerted its political strength. But it failed to experience a "revolution" against the proprietors to match that of South Carolina in 1719, or even to capture the mood held by its sister colony in the struggle after 1690.

In 1701 a colonial faction with firm ties to the Anglican church secured control of the Assembly by employing, as described by Henderson Walker, president of the Council, acting governor and a moderate churchman, "a great deal of care and management." This Assembly passed the First Vestry Act by a narrow margin. Although the specific content of the act is unknown, it apparently included the founding of parishes, the organization of vestries, the building of churches, and the levying of taxes to maintain the clergy. In brief, it embraced the prerequisites to institute a comprehensive church-state establishment.[39]

Walker, who had lived in Carolina for more than a decade, tried to implement the act, but those who opposed a church establishment rallied to repeal the act or at least to modify it. Quakers were the principal opponents, but they were reinforced by others. In reporting to the Society for the Propagation of the Gospel in Foreign Parts in 1703, John Blair wrote of distinct categories in the antiestablishment camp:

> First, the Quakers, who are the most powerful enemies to Church government, but a people very ignorant of what they profess. The second sort are a great many who have no religion, but would be Quakers, if by that they were not obliged to lead a more moral life than they are willing to comply to. A third sort are something like Presbyterians, which sort is upheld by some idle fellows who have left their lawful employment, and preach and baptize through the country, without any manner of orders from any sect of pretended Church.

Blair then described the proponents of the establishment, "who are really zealous for the interest of the Church, are the fewest in number, but the better sort of people, and would do very much for the settlement of the Church government there, if not opposed by these three precedent sects."[40]

In 1703 the opponents of the Vestry Act gained control of the Assembly. "My Lord," wrote Walker to the Bishop of

London, "I humbly beg leave to inform you, that we have an Assembly to sit the 3d November next, and there is above one half of the burgesses that are chosen are Quakers, and have declared their designs of making void the act for establishing the Church." The leaders of the Assembly intended to repeal the Vestry Act; but, unknowingly, this task was accomplished by the proprietors who had already declared the legislation invalid, not because they disapproved of an Anglican church establishment but because the act failed to provide adequate support for the clergy. John Blair reported that "the Quakers . . . will endeavor to prevent any such law passing for the future, for they are the greatest number in the Assembly, and are unanimous." [41]

The dispute over an Anglican church establishment had not, obviously, run its full course. Robert Daniel, resident of South Carolina and an ardent Church of England man, was appointed deputy governor by Governor Nathaniel Johnson upon the death of Henderson Walker in 1704. By that date the issue was further complicated because of the confrontation of establishment and antiestablishment forces in South Carolina. When the North Carolina Assembly met in March 1704, Daniel was fortified with special instructions to obtain an Establishment Act. He pressed for legislation to provide maintenance of an Anglican clergyman, but the Quaker-controlled Assembly refused to comply. [42]

Governor Daniel then attempted to oust the Quakers from the Assembly. His weapon was an act that required the taking of an oath of allegiance adopted by the English Parliament in the first year of the reign of Queen Anne. The Quakers, as a matter of faith, refused to take oaths and in many colonies were excused. Until Governor Daniel forced the issue, Quakers in North Carolina were not required to take oaths because to enforce compliance would automatically disqualify them from office. According to an account written five years later by William Gordon, an Anglican missionary, "the Quakers refusing to take [the Oath], they were dismissed [from] the council, Assembly, and courts of justice, and a law was made that none should bear any office or place of trust without taking such oaths." This maneuver gave the establishment forces a narrow majority—reportedly at most two votes. A Second Vestry Act was adopted whose precise language is not known because the document is not extant.[43]

Turbulent is the only adjective to describe North Carolina politics in the succeeding years as the respective partisans organized to gain control of the Assembly. The precise details are unknown because of insufficient records, but the two major factions continued to be Quaker-centered and Anglican-centered. The uncommitted were placed in a strategic role, but the evidence is not clear whether or not they recognized their advantage or whether they merely accepted the rule of the group temporarily in the ascendancy.

In this turmoil the labels "Quaker" and "Anglican" are misleading, because they imply that the struggle for power was a contest between religious factions and that each political bloc, in essence, constituted a closed circle. Somewhat surprisingly, the men supported by the Quaker bloc for the highest political offices within the colony were often Anglicans. To cite a prominent example, Edward Moseley served on one of the Anglican vestries, but he invariably was supported by the Quaker-dominated Assembly for the position of speaker, the highest office within the gift of the Assembly. Thomas Cary, whom the Quakers supported intermittently for governor, was also an Anglican churchman and appears to have been the same person who served as speaker of the Commons House of Assembly of South Carolina in 1707 and perhaps in the council of that colony in the 1690s.

In any case, the realities of politics are apparant. Political leaders recognized that acquiring control of the government carried with it desirable secular privileges which even a religious zealot could not treat lightly, and that these benefits could be shared. Colonial finances, for example, could be controlled by the Assembly using their power to name the public receiver. Religion-centered factions also recognized that influencing the governor had a direct relationship to the distribution of lands. Religious conviction cannot be dismissed as inconsequential, but neither can it be considered as the decisive factor in the political eruptions in North Carolina between 1704 and 1712.

Control of the government changed hands several times, often provoking violence. The Anglicans dominated the assembly affairs until 1708. In that election both parties claimed to be the legally elected representatives of the people, and each county sent two sets of delegates, one favoring the establishment and the other opposing it. The parties met in separate rooms, each claiming to be the authorized government. The Quakers, led by Edward Moseley, an Anglican, triumphed and Cary became governor while his opponent, William Glover, who at one stage had been supported by the Quakers but was now out of favor, fled to that favorite hideaway, Virginia.

The Cary-Moseley-Quaker alignment within the government was able to nullify the Test Oaths which had kept the Quakers out of the government, but in 1711, when the "Anglicans" regained control, the Quakers were brought to account. When Governor Edward Hyde arrived in January, he summoned an assembly in March that opposed the Cary-Moseley-Quaker position. The Reverend John Umrston[e], not always a particularly trustworthy witness because of a weakness for alcohol and his hatred of the Quakers, did, in this instance, describe the assembly with perspicacity: "A strange mixture of men of various opinions and inclinations a few Churchmen many Presbyterians Independents but most anythingarians some out of principle others out of hopes of power and authority in the Government to the end that they might Lord it over their Neighbours, all conspired to act answerable to the desire of the President of the council." [44]

But the Assembly was obviously more anti-Quaker than anything else, and it adopted a number of the pernicious enactments. All acts passed during the Cary-Moseley-Quaker period, 1708–1711, including all judicial proceedings, were nullified. The most extreme measure adopted by the Assembly was a sedition act that threatened to fine, imprison, and exclude from government those who uttered libel against the government. As is so often the case in sedition laws, the authors of the act were also to judge its infringement. Even Governor Spotswood of Virginia, from whom the Hyde government could expect support, observed: "It must be confessed they [the Hyde administration] shewed more their resentment of their ill usage during Mr. Cary's usurpation (as they call it) than their prudence to reconcile the distractions of the Country." [45]

Whereas Cary had been bereft of support because of popular expectations from Hyde, the sedition law and other punitive legislation raised a new protest from the colonials, especially the Quakers. Cary was determined to resist the execution of the laws. When Governor Hyde sent out a force to capture Cary, they found it impracticable because he had converted his house into an armed camp. When Hyde's forces retreated, Cary took the offensive and proceeded to attack Hyde. The "Cary Rebellion" of July 1711 was finally quelled when Governor Spotswood of Virginia sent a detachment of Royal Marines to assist Hyde. According to contemporary accounts, the Marines "frighted the Rebellious party so as to lay down their arms and disperse." Cary and his closest followers hastened to Virginia where they were imprisoned, sent to England for trial, and eventually released.[46]

In September the Tuscarora Indian War erupted and numerous outlying settlements in North Carolina were destroyed, their inhabitants massacred. Aid from South Carolina in the form of a force of whites and Indians headed by John "Tuscarora Jack" Barnwell saved the North Carolinians from further Indian attacks, and a second expedition in 1712 headed by James Moore, Jr., routed the Tuscaroras.

Somewhat chastened by the bloody encounter with neighboring Indians, North Carolina entered a more tranquil period. A new governor, Charles Eden, was appointed in 1714. A code of laws was adopted in 1715 which reflected a more orderly political structure. Among these laws was one which created an Anglican church establishment. Another enactment, "An Act for Liberty of Conscience," allowed Quakers and Dissenters the right to affirm rather than to subscribe to an oath. The willingness to accept the church establishment is perhaps the best evidence of the true weakness of the Anglican church. All questions had not been finally resolved, but North Carolina was slowly gathering sufficient political and economic strength to discard the proprietors and thereby to open a new phase in its history.

VI

In discussing the evolving political mosaic in the Carolinas, the contribution of local government or its absence has not yet been properly explored. In the Albemarle settlements that became North Carolina, local government flourished. In the Ashley River settlements that became South Carolina, every effort to establish local government failed. As early as 1664 the Carolina proprietors organized Albemarle and Clarendon counties; the former thrived but the latter did not. The designation given, that is, counties, was not, in reality, organized local government, but their subdivisions, called precincts, were.[47]

The date during the proprietary period when the precinct courts were officially recognized as agents of local government cannot be fixed, but the evidence is unmistakable
that they were fulfilling this obligation during the 1690s
and probably at least a decade earlier. The court minutes of
Perquimans precinct from February 1689 to April 1693 are
preserved, and the court's jurisdiction in all criminal cases,
excepting treason, murder, and other offences involving the
death penalty and civil cases not exceeding fifty pounds
sterling, was reaffirmed rather than created.[48]

To the four original Albemarle precincts operating by
1700—Perquimans, Currituck, Pasquotank, and Chowan—
two were added during the proprietary period: Bertie (1722)
and Tyrrell (1729). Five precincts—Beaufort, Hyde, Craven, Carteret, and New Hanover—made up Bath County,
created in 1696. In each original precinct a court functioned
with justices of the peace, usually four or five, but the number varied, with one serving as "stewart," a title derived
from the Fundamental Constitutions. A quorum was usually
required in order to conduct business. The jurisdiction regarding criminal cases remained unchanged, but the limit
of civil suits was adjusted from fifty pounds sterling to one
hundred pounds currency. Precinct courts were required
to meet four times a year, but some met more often, depending on the number of items on the docket. They served as
courts of record for the probation of wills and the register-
ing of deeds, mortgages, and conveyances as well as the re-
cording of births, marriages, and deaths. These courts fulfilled social responsibilities, such as the care of orphans and
the indigent, the supervision of violations involving inden-
tured servants and slaves, and the management of roads,
bridges, and ferries.[49]

The earliest records refer to a sheriff and constable to
execute court orders. In 1694 the title of sheriff was abandoned and that of provost marshall introduced, a title once

employed in Virginia. In practice the titles of sheriff and provost marshall became interchangeable. Precincts also became the unit of representation in the colonial assembly.

The political turbulence that gripped North Carolina at intervals during the proprietary period does not appear to have disrupted precinct, that is, local, government. Indeed, its operations were vastly strengthened, so that local government continued uninterrupted when North Carolina became a royal colony.

How different the story was in South Carolina! Representation from the respective counties, each with its clearly identified constituency, formed the base of power for political control of the colony. But no genuine effort was made during the proprietary period to establish local government, complete with court systems and magistrates with defined spheres of authority. Moreover, no serious consideration was given to provide a system of local government to fulfill such social obligations as care of the indigent and orphans, or to act as courts of record.

It is true that in 1720 the South Carolina Assembly, in a comprehensive petition to the Crown, listed the absence of local courts as one of the numerous grievances nursed by the colonials against the proprietors. "Neither have they settled any County jurisdiction for the preservation of the peace and regular Government according to the laws of England," asserted the petition, ". . . but have abandoned all to an unacountable disorder and confusion under the administracon and underhand management of a single person whom they have commissionated and call Chief Justice," the last reference, of course, directed to Nicholas Trott. The chief justice, the petition continued, holds "all Assize County Courts and Sessions only in Charles Town the only place of Judicature in the whole Province . . . summoning all persons from the remotest parts of the Colony to attend his Courts," from which there was no appeal. The case made by the petition of South Carolina was essentially a negative one, directed against Nicholas Trott rather than one which claimed that somehow serious neglect by the proprietors or their own shortsightedness failed to organize a systematic framework of local government, complete with county courts.[50]

When Francis Nicholson appeared in 1721 as the first royal governor, he recommended and the Commons House adopted legislation establishing county governments fashioned after the pattern of Virginia. But these governments never fulfilled the expectations of their creators, and before the decade of the 1720s closed all pretence of active county governments was dropped, never to be revived. Parishes took on certain social functions such as those affecting the poor, but county government and courts as they were known in North Carolina had no counterpart in South Carolina.[51]

Why were these end products of the two Carolinas so different when seemingly they had been subject to precisely the same rules, first under the proprietors and then the Crown? Demography unquestionably played a part—the dispersed settlements in North Carolina in contrast to the concentration of population along the Ashley and Cooper rivers with their respective tributaries—but that is by no means a complete or satisfactory answer. The pull of Charleston as a social-economic center with concentrated political influence also contributed to the centralizing rather than the decentralizing forces.

But a more profound political influence has generally escaped scholarly attention. The Albemarle settlements— North Carolina—accepted the Fundamental Constitutions with minor modifications as their governmental charter, and the Fundamental Constitutions provided for precinct, that is, local, government. All the functions of such an institution were prescribed: the precinct courts, the number of magistrates, the authority to be exercised by the magistrates, the limits of that authority, in brief, a comprehensive system of local government. "And you are to keepe or cause to be kept," proclaimed the Fundamental Constitutions, "ye sd Courts as often as by ye Fundamentall Constitutions is prescribed." In creating local governments, the Fundamental Constitutions dramatically influenced the institutions and practice of government in North Carolina.[52]

In direct contrast, South Carolina never accepted the Fundamental Constitutions as its charter of government, and its struggle against proprietary control from 1690 to 1700 was never duplicated in North Carolina. Local government as defined in the Fundamental Constitutions was never introduced into South Carolina, therefore, because it would have been considered a breach of principle, that only the colonists could decide such a question. No one can state with confidence why the settlers of South Carolina themselves failed to institute local government, but the political reality, that control of the assembly constituted control of colonial policy affecting each of the three counties, tended to place local government on a much lower order of priority during the proprietary period.

As a result, highly centralized government took deep root. When up-country Carolina grievances were articulated late in the colonial period, including the absence of local government which was a serious hardship for those remote from Charleston, it was too late to adjust a framework of political institutions and a political system whose shape had been formed during the proprietary period.

One final obvious, but pertinent, question relating to the political mosaic of the Carolinas remains to be asked: Why was the colony ultimately divided into North and South Carolina? A full answer requires a separate essay, especially when an examination of the historical literature reveals that no scholar has addressed the question, presumably on the assumption that the outcome was somehow inevitable.

But this response is unacceptable. After taking account of the geographic and demographic factors and noting the evolution of a small planter economy, what can be said, in light of the investigations into the early politics of the Carolinas, is that the division that was made had a pervasive, perhaps decisive, political component arising out of individual political experiences, which is another way of reasserting the significance of differing patterns of life and politics in the colonial South.

THREE

Reassessing the Founding of Georgia:

Enrichment of the Social Mosaic

FEW EPISODES IN THE HISTORY OF THE BRITISH COLONIES IN North America received more loving attention from the English poets of the eighteenth century than the early years of the founding of Georgia. Figures no less than Alexander Pope celebrated either the virtues of the infant settlement or its preeminent founder, James Oglethorpe; yet it was a lesser poet of pedestrian verse whose enthusiasms captured the image of a future, vibrant with hope:

> With nobler Products see thy *Georgia* teems!
> Chear'd with the genial Sun's directer Beams;
> Here the wild Vine to Culture learns to yield,
> And purple Clusters ripen thro' the Field.
> . . . Nor less the Care
> Of thy young Province to oblige the Fair:
> Here tend the Silkworm in the verdant Shade
> The frugal Matron, and the blooming Maid.[1]

In reality the founding of Georgia was a far more complicated operation than idyllic rhymes, sung by the poets, would lead one to believe, as its historians, following the lead of the participants, have since discovered. Some of the popular images, however, die hard. Largely independent from the Crown in managing the internal affairs of the

colony, the Trustees of Georgia received more financial assistance from Parliament than any other colony, proprietary
or royal—130,000 pounds sterling according to Percy Scott
Flippen. Idealism and humanitarianism supposedly moti-
vated the settlement and yet, in sustaining these objectives,
the Georgia trustees and their agents in the colony were
frequently despotic, and, in the eyes of some critics, tyrannical. Established as a haven for the impoverished debtors
from English prisons, Georgia achieved its highest distinction as a refuge for the oppressed of Europe. Moreover, the
number of men and women who financed their own under-
taking was sufficient to influence, indeed, finally to alter
dramatically, the entire development of the colony. As an
awed passenger aboard the *Anne*, the first ship to Georgia,
remarked: "We have five or six familys amongst us that are
deserving a Gentleman's Conversation." [2]

Although it was the southern outpost of the British continental colonies, Georgia did not resemble or develop in a
pattern typical of the frontier. Welcomed by South Carolina as a buffer against Spanish and French expansion in the
North American continent, the colony became an unwel-
come competitor for the lucrative fur trade and a source of
dismay in its operations against Spanish Florida. Here was a
colony, reputedly created in large measure to serve the ends
of humanity and philanthropy, which, in practice, served as
a lethal weapon poised to strike at European rivals of Britain with possessions on the North American continent.

I

Although the first settlers reached Charleston in January
1733 and the plotting out of Savannah on Yamacraw Bluff
took place in February of the same year, the founding of
Georgia emerged out of a complex background. One significant strand emanated from the establishment in 1728 of a

committee in Parliament entitled "The Committee to In-
quire into the State of the Gaols."

Its chairman was James Oglethorpe, a military man who,
for the eighteenth century, possessed in equal parts an enviable family history and influence with men whose power
and position were superior to his. Although destined to be
recorded as the founder of Georgia, Oglethorpe, with his
complex personality and the comfortable status that six centuries of sustained family prominence and activity could
bestow, seemed an unlikely prospect for such an under-
taking. Why should he leave familiar scenes where his worth
was recognized to enter an environment largely unknown?
Was not this a task for men of lesser standing? To employ
one's influence in the cause of settlement was one thing, but
to participate was quite another.

Historians have learned, however, that Oglethorpe was
not a pliable personality, animated solely by good works and
high intentions, but an unyielding, often difficult person,
demanding and imperious. His record as chairman of the
Committee on the Gaols has been justifiably remembered,
but the quick temper which twice provoked him to draw
his sword against defenseless men has been mercifully for-
gotten. Perhaps Oglethorpe's display of an inner ironlike
discipline originated in misgivings for his early excesses. No
one can deny his courage, but his judgment is open to
question. Single-mindedness, often an invaluable asset in
the lives of great men, in Oglethorpe's case blinded him to
reality and led him to the brink of disaster. But Oglethorpe
recovered from disaster. He lived to become a legend and
to witness the emergence of the royal colony of Georgia, for
which he expressed no interest, survive a revolution and
become an integral part of a new nation.[3]

The Committee on the Gaols, in making its report with
its detailed description of filth, ill treatment, graft, and generally deplorable conditions, pricked the English compla-

cency of the eighteenth century. Parliament swiftly adopted
an enactment in 1730 that freed many debtors who had
been thrown into prison for trivial offenses. Equally if not
more important, leading statesmen began to consider
whether the nation was being properly served when able-
bodied, capable men wasted their energies under debilitat-
ing circumstances. Under proper conditions, their efforts
could be made to improve not only their own lot but also
the wealth, power, and prestige of the nation. So wrote
Joshua Gee, a prominent political economist, in his *The
Trade and Navigation of Great Britain Considered*, recommending that "useless people," including those reduced to
poverty, would be of greater value to the nation appropri-
ately employed in the colonies. Gee's arguments were not
lost on the Georgia founders, and as a consequence two separate ideas were joined in common cause, the humanitarian
impulse to help the indigent and the compelling mercan-
tilistic aspiration to profit the nation.

The philanthropic thrust did not operate indiscriminate-
ly; it was channeled through the specific agency of the Associates of Thomas Bray. Dr. Bray was well known in the
southern colonies for his active part in the Society for the
Propagation of the Gospel in Foreign Parts and for his service in sending libraries to the colonies in North America.
The Associates of Bray had been formed to administer a
charitable trust. Bray sought out Oglethorpe after the latter
won national recognition as chairman of the Gaols Committee. The Associates of Bray, together with the support
of prominent members of the Committee on the Gaols, were
utilized by Oglethorpe and others to reinforce the drive to
found a colony on the southern frontier to be called Georgia.

The Georgia charter was granted in June 1732, although
the application had been in process for some two years.
Originally the document included the names of twenty-one
men called trustees. Easily the most familiar were Ogle-

thorpe, James Vernon, connected with the leading families of England, and John, Viscount Percival, who would soon receive a title as the first Earl of Egmont. The charter forbade the trustees from obtaining any land in Georgia, a clause that Parliament insisted should be inserted. It also created a simple governing organization, a Common Council among the trustees, which, unlike any other English colony in North America, kept governance for all practical purposes within England. Most influential members among the trustees were also members of Parliament, which proved to be advantageous during the desperate early decades.[4]

The establishment of Georgia is so well known that we tend to overlook the fact that it is unique in the history of the English colonization of North America, another piece of the mosaic reflecting the character of the colonial South. Its form, functions, source of authority, and directed objectives, considered together, have no counterpart elsewhere in the British empire.

Scholars have disagreed on two questions that involve the development preceding actual settlement. It has been asserted that the Bray associates should properly be thought of as the genesis of Georgia, but it has also been effectively argued that the men who became Bray associates were Parliament men first and associates second and that the idea of the colony of Georgia was conceived in their political capacities rather than in their philanthropic impulses.[5]

The second question is of far greater importance: What light do these events shed on the motivations of the founders of Georgia? Did official Britain wish to strengthen its position in the international competition with Spain and France? Was the colony truly designed to relieve the debtors recently released from English prisons? Or was the primary purpose to establish a settlement that could produce goods useful to the mother country but unavailable in other colonies?

Evidence can readily be advanced to support the validity of each motivating force, and certainly the founding of Georgia represented a fusion of various motives; but it becomes increasingly evident that Georgia's principal function was to act as a buffer against Spain and France. The word "defense" rings out incessantly in almost every significant extant document. Indeed, a case can be made that the establishment of Georgia is a singular instance, with the possible exception of Virginia, in which a decision to plant a colony was based primarily on imperial rather than mercantile considerations.

The creation of a model community to suit, so it was thought, the needs and designs of the empire or the objectives of a group of farsighted trustees in England was decidedly a second order of priority.[6] In some respects, these two motivating factors did not conflict; certainly they were not wholly separated in the minds of the trustees, philanthropic enterprise being so rare in the secular mind of the eighteenth century that it required a somewhat exotic taste. But the final judgment must rest upon the execution of the task.

There can be no question whatever on one point: Georgia was not a colony composed of debtors taken from the prisons of England. There remains the possibility—one that is impossible to check—that some of the earlier settlers, sent at the expense of the trustees, were selected from those who were released from prison in 1730 several years before the colony was established. Generally, however, Georgia was composed of a great diversity of people, each group with its special motivation, interests, and goals, a circumstance that, more than any single factor, accounts for the sharp conflicts that arose within the colony which finally transformed it from a flawed trusteeship into a flourishing possession of the Crown.

II

What these broad differences demonstrate is that, contrary to assumptions generally advanced, no single unitary plan for Georgia, much less a "grand design," ever existed. No scholar has perceived this more clearly than Paul Taylor in his thoughtful study entitled *Georgia Plan: 1732–1752.* "The plan was not monolithic," he writes. "The motivations and purposes of the trustees as individuals had much in common, but they were not identical." Quoting a single contemporary source, Taylor does conclude that the prohibition of slavery served as the "fundamental" core of the Georgia plan, a challenging but not wholly convincing thesis.[7]

Taylor understates rather than overstates the case against the existence of a Georgia plan. The record reveals that each trustee had his own image of what the focus of the enterprise should be. For Thomas Coran it represented an opportunity to advance religion; Lord Egmont believed the colony could be molded into a model society; James Vernon became the spokesman for policies simply to encourage a flourishing colony; and James Oglethorpe regarded the Georgia settlement fundamentally as an outpost of empire. The colony had no contemporary collective image. Historians created it, and textbooks have popularized it.

In any discussion of the trusteeship period the three celebrated restrictive policies affecting the colony are mistakenly offered as convincing evidence of a grand design for Georgia: forbidding the use of rum; a land policy limiting ownership to no more than five hundred acres with a qualifying covenant, *tale male*, meaning only males could inherit; and finally, the prohibition of slavery. In themselves these policies do not constitute a plan, because they do not inform us as to the objectives these policies were expected to achieve. Why forbid the use of rum? Why restrict land policy? Why prohibit slavery?

These queries raise a barrage of fresh questions requiring intelligent and documented responses. Was rum prohibited because Oglethorpe believed it made settlers, but more particularly soldiers, ill, and thus diminished the defense posture? Or was policy on rum adopted because of the fear that its use would invite slave merchants into Georgia? The correspondence between Oglethorpe and other agents in Georgia repeatedly reveals complaints of the consumption of rum. When the act was adopted in April 1735 to prohibit importation and use of rum and brandy, its preamble focused on the "hurtful" and "pernicious" effects on health which could ruin the colony. Neither the early restrictions on rum nor the specific act prevented its continuous use.[8]

Were the restrictions on land a mechanism to strengthen the defense of Georgia for the inevitable confrontation with Spain and France? Oglethorpe asserted that a settler automatically became a member of the militia, and a grant of land involved a military commitment. "And as the Military Strength of the Province was particularly to be taken care of; it seemed necessary to establish such Tenures of Lands; as might most effectively preserve the Number of Lots of Land; and therefore each Lot of Land was to be considered as a military Fief," he wrote. Because women could not serve as soldiers—"for Women being equally incapable to serve on Juries as to act as soldiers"—they should not inherit the land.[9] Some trustees also argued that the land policy was instituted to prevent large planters from absorbing the property of small landholders so that neither the defenses would be weakened nor the agricultural experiments to produce exotic staples for export to England be undermined. It has also been asserted—and there is evidence to support this position—that the policies governing land grants served as a barrier to a plantation economy, based on slave labor. If so, was not defense again the underlying issue?

Indeed, the critical question arises whether slavery was prohibited because of moral and humanitarian considerations or because its presence weakened defenses. In the act adopted to prohibit slavery, the rationale was offered in the phrase: "An Act for rendering the Colony of Georgia more Defencible." The preamble is even more explicit:

> WHEREAS Experience hath Shewn that the manner of Settling Colonys and Plantations with Black Slaves or Negroes hath Obstructed the Increase of English and Christian Inhabitants therein who alone can in case of a War be relyed on for the Defence and Security of the same, and hath Exposed the colonys so settled to the Insurrections Tumults and Rebellions of such Slaves & Negroes and in Case of a Rupture with any Foreign State who should Encourage and Support such Rebellions might Occasion the utter Ruin and loss of such Colony, For the preventing therefore of so great inconveniences in the said Colony of Georgia We the Trustees

wish to prohibit blacks from entering the colony.[10]

Until Oglethorpe became wholly preoccupied with the founding of Georgia, he served as deputy-governor of the Royal African Company, an office that certainly appears incompatible with a stance that slavery was unjust and morally wrong. Oglethorpe repeatedly argued against slaves as a labor force because they would weaken Georgia's defensive position as an outpost of empire, and a diligent search of his writings fails to reveal a clear-cut statement that he regarded slavery as inhuman or immoral. The historian is hard pressed to discover any of the trustees, including Egmont, finding slavery to be morally wrong or socially repellent. It is illuminating that when the affairs of Georgia reached their most urgent crisis in 1741–1742 and its fate was being debated by Parliament, Lord Egmont, in a personal letter to Oglethorpe revealing his most intimate thoughts, did not speak of the colony as a social experiment, a model society, or charitable enterprise but rather as the cornerstone of British interest in confrontation with its international rivals:

> The Colony is this day undone, for upon presenting our Petition and the Motion to refer it to the committee, Sr. John Hynd Cotton divided the House and it was carried by 13 not to refer it. We intend if possible to recover it, but it is doubtfull. Mr. Verelst will write you more upon it; Such Ignorance of Great Britains true Interest, in giving up a Province without one Word of debate, and such breach of Publick Fath [*sic*] to the poor Foreigners and natural born Subjects must Surprize all Europe, and rejoyce the Spaniards. The Carolinians may triumph in annexing Georgia again to their province, for that must be the Consequence, (if not retrievable) and our Clamarous Malecontents may rejoice to be Subjects under them, but I question whether Carolina will not be urgent for as great sums to defend her self now this Barrier is gone.[11]

Only the Salzburgers found the slave system extremely distasteful when they first witnessed its operation in South Carolina.[12]

What one must conclude is that not only was there no uniform "grand design" for Georgia, but also that the objective of the three policies considered to be the core of the comprehensive plan can be variously interpreted. This observation seriously undermines the assertion, perhaps most felicitously articulated by Daniel Boorstin, that the Georgia plan, conceived in England without regard to the American environment, foundered on the shoals of reality in the New World—a classic example of Old World ideas becoming obsolete when transplanted to the American wilderness. Indeed, the so-called plan for Georgia did not need to traverse the Atlantic to fail, if "fail" is the appropriate word. The absence of a clear definition of objectives by those who advocated the establishment of the colony and controlled its development was destined to result in unrealized expectations in Georgia, in England, or any other territory on earth.

III

The so-called Georgia plan, ill-defined, especially in terms of its goals, was even further distorted in its execution. The first group of colonists, led by General Oglethorpe who volunteered to accompany the expedition, sailed from Gravesend in England in the *Anne*, a stout ship of two hundred tons, owned in part by Samuel Wragg of London, with John Thomas, master, to arrive in Charleston harbor 13 January 1733.[13] Governor Robert Johnson of South Carolina had warned Oglethorpe to "send none but People used to Labour and of Sober Life and Conversation, for others will never be govern'd nor make good Settlers, for much hardship, sickness and Labour will attend their first Settling, which will not be born by People used to Idleness or Luxury, and So far from being thankfull for the Bounty bestowed upon them, will be discontended and mutinous." [14] His note of caution arrived too late, for the expedition was already on the Atlantic; yet the group was described as "sober, industrious, and moral men," one hundred and more first settlers equipped with a variety of skills. Unfortunately, as the record proved and the lists of passengers showed, too many lacked experience in the most desirable skill of all—farming. It was a handicap that was not easily overcome.[15]

The future Georgians were warmly welcomed by the citizens of South Carolina, for that colony saw beyond any charitable settlement to the ultimate purpose of establishing a shield between Carolina and Spanish Florida. Carolina gave money and provisions, more than a hundred breeding cattle no less, to assist in the founding of Georgia, and sent some of its most prominent and experienced leaders, such as William Bull and James St. Julian, to advise Oglethorpe in laying out a settlement, a suggestion made earlier by Governor Johnson. Ironically, in view of Georgia's intended prohibition of slavery, black slaves from South Carolina were employed in the first months of the settlement—by order of the trustees—to assist in clearing land and in constructing buildings. The hospitality of Carolina was eventually to wear thin when it realized that the new colony might interfere with its Indian trade or, even later, when the valor of Carolinians was challenged in a campaign against Spanish Florida. But in February 1733 spring was approaching; no one could foresee the future. Fractious thoughts and discord seemed remote.[16]

Oglethorpe's first task was to establish friendly relations with the Indians in the area. In this he was eminently successful, in part because the tribe nearest the proposed settlement was a frail castoff from the mighty Creek Nation. "They [the Indians] came to bid us welcome," wrote one of the settlers, "and before them came a Man dancing in Antick Postures with a spread Fan," a token of friendship. After the dance was completed, accompanied by a "very uncouth Hollowing," the Indians approached Oglethorpe's tent where they were hospitably treated and presented with gifts.[17]

An agreement was drawn up giving the land to the English, a pretense of legal fiction that was so often scrupulously observed in the English colonies only to be grossly violated as the pressure to move inland mounted. According to one report, the chief, Tomochichi, attended church services. Certainly Tomochichi remained a firm friend of Oglethorpe, in part because of his dependence for supplies and provisions from the trustees' store. Whether Tomochichi was rewarded in the afterlife will forever remain a mystery, but upon his death his station among whites was duly recognized; at his own request he was buried with ceremony in a prominent square in Savannah. A failure among the red men, Tomochichi was content to accept his new status among the whites.

Peaceful relations having been established with the Indians, Oglethorpe set in motion a plan for settlement on Yamacraw Bluff, a site that towered some thirty to forty yards above the river. Savannah, for so the settlement was named, was laid out in a regular pattern with lots measuring approximately twenty yards by thirty yards, although some of the lots, according to complaints made later, were laid off in a triangular fashion. The colonists first lived in tents, but small single-story frame houses were begun, measuring eight paces by five paces. Garrets, the space between the ceiling and roof joists, were made habitable. One observer reported that most of the first houses were raised two feet above the ground and floored with one-and-a-half-inch plank. Primitive fortifications were quickly erected; indeed, they took priority, another manifestation of Oglethorpe's anxious concern that the Spanish were looking over his shoulder.

Oglethorpe's concept of the extent of Georgia in a rather surprising way was imperfect. The territory south of the Savannah River had been subject to dispute between Spain and Britain for centuries. At one time Spain held the view that Georgia was not only a part of its dominion but much of the Carolinas as well. In view of Oglethorpe's military background, it would be assumed that his knowledge of the region would have been precise, based on the best available materials. Yet, upon his arrival, Oglethorpe confessed to his fellow trustees: "This Province is much larger than we thought it, being 120 Miles from this River [the Savannah] to the Alatamaha." [18]

After a few months Oglethorpe left the colony for Charleston to make arrangements for provisions and other supplies. Upon returning to Savannah in August 1733, Oglethorpe found the colonists "grown very mutinous and impatient of Labour and Discipline." He declared that "some of the Silly People desired their Provisions that they might be able to gratify their Palates by Selling a large Quantity of wholesome food for a little Rum Punch." Oglethorpe found it difficult to revive what he called the spirit of labor, but "by Degrees" he "brought the People to Discipline." The cause of the trouble, Oglethorpe was convinced, was the use of rum.[19]

But the future of Georgia and its character as a colony depended primarily on the type of settlers whom Oglethorpe and the trustees enlisted in their enterprise. Somehow this essential factor seemed never to be fully recognized. As a result people whose expectations differed dramatically from those of the trustees were encouraged to come, thereby planting the thorn of discord with the seed of life.

The first group to be considered in the category were those people of British extraction sent at the expense of the trustees, estimated at more than seven hundred souls in the first five years of settlement. According to the lists which serve as a partial inventory of personnel, the occupations and backgrounds of these individuals varied greatly—from surgeons and apothecaries to peruke-makers and carpenters. What they needed most they lacked—a common ideal to match the image, or, more accurately, the multiplicity of images, of Georgia envisioned by the trustees. A fatal flaw remained undetected when the trustees assumed that other men, in agreeing to settle in Georgia, automatically shared a set of ideas that they were willing to transform into reality.

Two other groups to appear shortly after the first settlement were the Irish convicts and the Moravians. Widely different in background and conviction, they shared the experience of being equally hostile to key concepts of what the Georgia settlement was intended to be.

A boatload of Irish convicts was purchased by Oglethorpe when a vessel, originally destined for another port, entered the Savannah River. Of course, Oglethorpe had the best of intentions: he needed workmen to clear the land and to cultivate the soil. Following the precedent set by his fellow trustees, Oglethorpe neglected to ask himself whether a model community could be established without the assurance that all hands wished to pursue a particular objective. The Irish convicts, some of whom contributed to the well-being of the settlement and others who caused discord, were not consulted on whether they found the goals of the trustees attractive or even desirable. As a group, the instinct of these convicts for survival, regardless of artificially established policies, thwarted the aims of the colony.

From a different vantage point, the same observation holds for the Moravians. Fleeing to the New World to escape the disharmony and conflict of the Old World, the Moravians, who held firmly to the pacifist position that taking up arms was dishonoring God, were poorly equipped to settle in a community whose watchword was defense and one of whose principal purposes was to confront the enemy. Guided by their consciences, dismayed with their economic prospects in Georgia, and attracted by the rolling countryside in Pennsylvania, the Moravians, in contrast to the convicts who had no choice, left Georgia, their presence unmarked except for a few epitaphs.[20]

Forty Jewish settlers, a project underwritten financially by a group of wealthy Jews in London, arrived quite unexpectedly in Georgia in the summer of 1733. Governor Johnson of South Carolina was alarmed. "We cannot fathom," he wrote, "the Design of sending forty Jews to Georgia, they will never I believe make Planters." [21] Although ad-

vised by the trustees to ask them to leave the colony, Oglethorpe welcomed them. A number of the original Jewish
contingent failed, but others weathered the first stormy decades of settlement. Their names never appeared on the petitions from the dissatisfied elements, not because they were
content but because the petitioners were afraid their case
might be prejudiced if Jewish names were included. Because
property restrictions were practiced against Jews in many
countries in the eighteenth century, the land restrictions in
Georgia may have appeared less offensive to the Jewish settlers than to the other colonials.

Finally, there were two additional clusters of Georgia
settlers so different in motivation that they neatly illustrate
the cleft between those who could accommodate themselves
to the aims of the settlement and those who could not, in the
first case because the ends they were seeking did not directly
contradict those of the trustees while, in the second case,
they did. The Salzburgers from Germany, who introduced
a new element into the Georgia colonization scheme, constituted the first group. The second group is commonly
called adventurers, men of differing backgrounds who came
to Georgia on their own account, usually carrying with
them a number of servants and often receiving large grants
of land. Their aim: to become commercial planters.

As early as 1732 adventurers were introduced into the
colonizing scheme of Georgia, thus injecting a potent divi-
sive force in the so-called grand design. When their numbers were augumented during the first half decade, this division was merely accented, as events were to prove; yet
Oglethorpe, as late as 1736, failed to perceive the obvious
collision between the aims of the trustees and the goals of
the adventurers, for he suggested that the Trust send additional "gentlemen" as well as four hundred servants.

These adventurers, the gentlemen of early Georgia, have
not received the attention that is due a group which best

explains why the colony failed to live up to its expectations.
Not poverty-ridden tradesmen or toil-worn farmers, these
men assumed that their high status would entitle them to
special rewards. Individuals brought to the colonies by the
grace of the trustees might accept trustee regulation, but
gentlemen accustomed to favored treatment were not so
eager or prepared to conform, particularly if a conflict of
interests were to arise; and the adventurers had neither a
desire to create an outpost of empire that could defy the
French and Spanish, nor a particular stake in establishing a
model community, either for defense or charity. The adventurers sought economic opportunities, and they were willing to invest their own money in hope of substantial returns.
A policy that interfered with this ultimate goal became
an undesirable threat. Therefore, if the consideration of
creating a special community is laid aside, the trustees'
policies with respect to land and slaves were, in effect, potential barriers to wealth and affluence, the essential objective of the adventurers.

As if this conflict of goals were not sufficient grounds for
a contest of wills, circumstances in the early stages of settlement widened the fissure between the trustees and their
generalized concept of the colony's future, and the adventurers and their concept of what actions should be taken.
According to letters they sent to the trustees soon after ar-
riving, several adventurers had expected to receive the same
encouragement that was given the colonists sent by the trustees: namely, provisions for themselves and their servants
for a period, preferably a year, and tools for building
houses, clearing the land, and cultivating the soil. None of
these benefits had been granted them. As a result, they were
compelled to expend capital from the beginning. Considering only the industrious adventurers, thus setting aside
those who were so dismayed at the outset that they failed
to cultivate their lands, their investments failed to bring a

reurn before their capital was exhausted, leaving them if
not destitute, certainly seriously reduced in circumstances.
That this outcome should awaken a clamor for a modification of existing trustee policies is scarcely surprising.

The first group of Salzburgers, whose methods and motivations stood in sharp contrast to the adventurers, arrived
in April 1734, although preparations had been made as
early as 1732. The Salzburgers' ranks were supplemented
in the years to follow, but as late as 1740, the Reverend John
Martin Bolzius, leader of the flock, reported that their settlement had not yet reached two hundred souls, a pitifully
small number in view of their arduous labor and the continuous support they received from the trustees. Despite
its slow development, however, this group must be considered the most successful settlement in Georgia.[22]

The Salzburgers were a devout group of Lutherans, who
had been driven from their homes in the Archbishopric of
Salzburg by an order from His Highness Leopold Anton
who, on 31 October 1732, Reformation Day, issued an edict
ordering all non-Catholics to leave the province within
three months and those holding no property to leave within
three days. It is estimated that more than thirty thousand
Protestants were affected by this decree. No more than four
score, urged on by Dr. Samuel Urlsperger of Augsburg and
the British Society of Christian Knowledge, originally sailed
for the New World. The Salzburgers were cordially welcomed in Georgia, greeted by the firing of cannon in their
honor and provided with a splendid banquet, creating a
festive air that did not prepare them for the disappoint-
ments that lay ahead.

Allotted a grant of land north and west of Savannah, the
Salzburgers called it Ebenezer. The soil proving sandy and
barren, the Salzburgers begged for permission to move.
John Vat, who accompanied the second group of Salzburgers, reported that the soil in the original settlement would

not yield a livelihood despite the most industrious effort and that the first Salzburger settlers were "exceedingly Struck down and dishearten'd." [23] The trustees were reluctant to allow the Salzburgers a new grant, for they realized that if a concession were made to the Salzburgers, it would invite petitions from everyone who was dissatisfied with his grant. Permission was finally secured in 1736, however, and the Salzburgers moved to Red Bluff, this time naming their settlement "New" Ebenezer, meaning new hope.

Although reinforced with members of their faith from Europe and consistently assisted by the trustees in obtaining provisions and other essentials by means of their store in Savannah, the lot of the Salzburgers was not a happy one. Their cattle herd dwindled and their crops failed. Only the will to create a Godly community as a supreme objective enabled them to endure hardships and sacrifices that others less patient or zealous would have found intolerable. They lived as a community. The men, for example, worked in the fields in groups, apparently in teams of six members. Jointly they cleared land and raised buildings. A single herdsman, with occasional help, cared for the livestock. Women and children were an integral part of the working community. Each evening, after the day's work was completed, the entire group assembled for worship services. Even with such devotion and labor, the Salzburgers would have starved without the necessities continually provided by the trustees, "being hitherto forced without their fault," wrote Bolzius in 1737, "to live from ye Trustee's Stores at Savannah." [24]

That the Salzburgers endured when other settlements in Georgia eventually collapsed is attributable to a number of factors. First, of course, they were aided with supplies and provisions from the trustees' store. Second, their desires tended to harmonize rather than conflict with those of many trustees. The Salzburgers were trying to create their own

model community, which, though it did not have defense
or other considerations of empire as its object, was based on
an ideal of mutual concern rather than individual entrepre-
neurship. Third, settling and working as a group rather
than individually made them a far more efficient economic
unit, in contrast to the other settlements in Georgia. Fourth,
their lack of political experience enabled them to accommodate to vigorous definition of policy by superiors without
the favor of consultation, a contrast to native Britons, particularly "gentlemen," who considered themselves as entitled to speak and act rather than merely listen and obey.
Fifth, of the trustees' policies most subject to criticism—the
prohibition of rum and slavery and the limited title to land
—only the last immediately affected the Salzburgers. Rum
was not important to a people with the convictions of the
Salzburgers—it was an inconsequential issue in any case—
and they managed to adjust to the problem of land titles in
part because of their distinctive group settlements. Introduction of slavery tended to undermine the ideals that the
Salzburgers carried to the New World; but by the 1750s,
when slaves were permitted, a number of them compromised, making modest fortunes as a result of using slave
labor. In such cases the urge to prosper overcame the commitment to an ideal.

Such diversity of goals among the settlers was seriously
complicated by the inability to meet the first requirement
of a new colony, an adequate food supply. The testimony
on this point is conclusive. The Salzburgers, for example,
failed to obtain so much as the return on their seed when
planting at Ebenezer. Hugh Anderson, a "gentleman" who
worked his land assiduously, became utterly discouraged
when his garden crops as well as his commercial undertak-
ings failed. As late as 1741 Oglethorpe remained dubious
regarding the ability of the colony to secure provisions. "I
think," he wrote, "I have got the people of Savannah on

Such a footing that they can now buy or raise their provisions." [25]

Subsistence itself, therefore, became a daily concern; finding a commercial crop, without which the future, particularly for adventurers, was limited, compounded the problem. The objective, as with most English colonies, had been to raise a product useful to Britain. Indeed, the trustees and some of the inhabitants looked upon this aspect of the settlement as a grand experiment. Vineyards, fruit trees, and cotton were planted, and lumbering as well as the production of pitch and tar were tried. Silk making in particular attracted every possible incentive: land was allocated on condition that a proportion be devoted to planting mulberry trees, the services of an artisan skilled in soil production were obtained, and subsidies were provided for finished silk. The trustees engaged botanists to sail to the Spanish Caribbean, assigning specific ports of call where exotic plants including a cinnamon tree were acquired and dispatched to Georgia. [26]

The soil of Georgia, however, did not cooperate. Early reports predicted glowing prospects, especially for silk; but most crops that were later to become such an important part of Georgia's economy, such as rice and cotton, lacked either the market or the proper conditions for growth. Promising crops that grew well in carefully tended gardens failed when the experiment was carried into the fields. Moreover, the shortage of labor limited the time and attention that could be given to any crop. In practice Georgia failed to solve its agriculture problem during most of the trustee period. Only dispensing provisions by the trustees' store prevented starvation. This practice departed from the original plan which had advocated supplying individuals brought over by the Trust for one year. The closing of the trustee's store in 1740 contributed substantially to the emerging crisis in the colony's affairs. [27]

As early as 1734 Thomas Christie, the recorder for the colony, recognized this problem and reported it to Oglethorpe. "All those Productions will be a Considerable time before they are brought to any Perfection and we shall be always Poor and Needy till we are able to make Exports of our Own." [28] This observation was to be repeated frequently in one form or another in subsequent years.

Indian trade served as the only immediate avenue of commerce. Because of the itinerant character of this activity, it, too, militated against the design of a stable, settled, compact community envisioned by the trustees. Preoccupied with defense, Oglethorpe and the trustees regarded the Indians largely in terms of military strategy rather than as an integral part of a flourishing economy. A policy on Indian trade, therefore, was not defined for several years, and remarkably few Georgians engaged in it.

IV

The faulty execution of a design that lacked clarity and uniformity in its conception resulted in predictable consequences, albeit an unforeseen social legacy. Dissatisfaction, articulate and broadly based, emerged. Rooted in social and economic discontent, the complaints became increasingly political in expression and content.

Politics in early Georgia remained remarkably uncomplicated; the trustees, in practice, retained total control. Within the body of the trustees, a Common Council, generally composed of the most active members of the group, customarily made the critical decisions. These decisions were translated into deeds when either the secretary, Benjamin Martyn, or the treasurer, Harman Verelst, issued instructions to an agent in the colony, Oglethorpe being the first. No form of either colonial or local government comparable to a colony such as Virginia or North Carolina ever existed.[29]

Oglethorpe returned to England several times between 1733 and 1740, leaving Thomas Causton in charge, invested with the title of chief magistrate as well as the trustees' storekeeper. As the dispenser of provisions as well as the dispenser of justice, Causton held an enviable position; this combination led to an abuse of power. In 1737 William Stephens was sent to Georgia by the trustees and designated as their secretary in Georgia. He also served them as a reporter, keeping a fulsome daily journal in which he recorded everything that happened. Causton was eventually removed from his position of eminence, to be replaced, at least in terms of the responsibilities of the foremost civil officer, by William Stephens. In this process Oglethorpe was gradually relieved of his authority in civil affairs, although his position as the military head of the colony was never questioned. For a brief period Oglethorpe was made the highest civil officer in Frederica, but he was ultimately displaced. Oglethorpe never fully accepted the changes made in the disposition of civil affairs by his fellow trustees; he always believed that the colony was most successful when he managed daily affairs single-handedly, unhampered by the few magistrates appointed by the trustees meeting in England.[30]

In effect, Georgia was subjected largely to one-man rule, as the trustees placed authority seriatim upon selected individuals, and it was not always the rule of the wise. The complaints against Causton, for example, were numerous. It was said that he used the goods and servants of the trustees for his own purposes and that his house was "well furnished with Plenty of every thing to Profuseness." [31] He abused his power as chief magistrate, wasting people's time with unnecessary ceremony to inflate his own importance. There is conclusive evidence that Causton was opening much, if not all, of the outgoing mail, thereby acting as a one-man censor. Whenever a complaint was forwarded by a settler, for instance, Causton's letter to the trustees of the same date would include answers to each specific charge.

By catering to some settlers and withholding from others, Causton built up a group of supporters. Eveleigh, the Carolina merchant, visiting Georgia in Oglethorpe's absence in 1735, found the people divided "like Court and Country in England." Eveleigh further observed that "the Magistrates and the better Sort" seemed to be on one side and the "Populacy . . . with a few of the better Sort on the other."[32] If such an alignment existed, it was shattered in the years to follow when the magistrates stood, for the most part, alone against the prominent spokesmen for the colony. At first Oglethorpe, with his prestige and his earnest desire to do justice, served as the safety valve for a dissatisfied populace, but his usefulness in this respect disappeared by 1738.

With the motivations and objectives of the people who settled in Georgia at such variance from those of the trustees, with the difficulty of raising sufficient provisions to maintain the settlement, and with the inability to produce a staple that could instill commercial life in the colony, it is small wonder that the Georgia outpost should be torn with dissension. The truth is that the colony, after the first enthusiasms of settlement had ebbed, was in serious trouble. The trustees were misled by taking the early descriptions of success literally, and this misconception was fed by the Salzburgers, who, when they sought additional help, adopted a subservient tone. "God reward You a thousand times for all your Goodness presented to us in the former time," their spiritual leader wrote in 1734. As a result, the trustees regarded any complaint with suspicion, the voice, so they deceived themselves, of chronic grumblers.[33]

By the late 1730s, however, the hardship and indicators

of failure were everywhere apparent, even to the officials who represented the trustees. Drought, illness, and the fear of invasion coupled with crop failures caused distress throughout the colony. The Salzburgers, the most successful group, found conditions depressing. Reverend Bolzius wrote in 1737, when a chilling despair was seeping into the settlement, that half of his group had died and the remaining half were hard pressed to survive. The Salzburgers could live, declared Bolzius, only through the goods supplied by the trustees' store.

Three years later, when conditions were approaching a crisis, George Whitefield, the celebrated preacher, thought it his "duty" to inform the trustees of the "declining state" of the colony, noting particularly the sad conditions of Frederica, Darien, and Savannah. Outlying settlements were abandoned. Although Savannah had given the appearance of relatively rapid growth because planters, having lost their capital, moved to town, it was estimated that by 1740 fully seventy houses were vacant. Whitefield claimed that without his pump priming activities in hiring men to build the Orphan House facilities, which he had established, conditions would have been even worse. James Habersham, left in charge of the Orphan House, reported to Whitefield: "Most of the Inhabitants, except the Saltsburghers having left the Colony, our Supplyes of that nature [provisions] are brought to us from other Provinces." [34] The trustees, by closing their store in 1740, inadvertently intensified the problem. "The people throughout the Province are discontented & uneasie," wrote a soldier stationed in the colony, "(not from any apprehensions from the Enemy)." [35]

The crisis that developed can be best traced through a series of letters and petitions to the trustees, beginning in 1735, and culminating in 1741 with the publication of *A True and Historical Narrative of the Colony of Georgia in America, From the First Settlement Thereof Until this*

Present Period; Containing the Most Authentic Facts, Matters, and Transactions Therein. . . . At the outset redress was directed to two requests: one, that a limited number of slaves be permitted in the colony; and two, that there be some alterations in land tenure. By 1740, however, when the dissatisfaction reached a crescendo, the emphasis was broadened to include: self-government; release from excessive quitrents; and the right to take up land where it was convenient rather than by trustee assignment, as well as the familiar issues of slaves and a more drastic change in land tenure. To appreciate the intensity of the movement for modification of trustee policy, it is well to underscore the transition from the limited objections of 1735 to the sweeping ones of 1741, and to note the marked increase in the proportion of colonists who were clamoring for some modification of policy.

Unfortunately, historians have employed the word "malcontents" or as contemporaries spelled it, "malecontents," to identify the advocates of change. This expression, used by agents of the trustees in the colony when writing their superiors to describe those who were dissatisfied with conditions as they existed, has a pejorative connotation. As such it does the movement an injustice, for it suggests that opponents of the trustees were ill-tempered men, unwilling to respond to the natural challenges of settlement, when, in reality, the dissatisfaction arose out of a fundamental conflict in goals. The trustees and a major proportion of the population had contradictory objectives, a problem exacerbated by an inability to solve the colony's economic problem and the absence of self-government.

In creating the myth that the malcontents were the cause rather than the result of conditions, historians have tended to follow the lead of contemporaries. William Stephens and Thomas Jones, for instance, two officials of the trustees in America as well as Lord Egmont, a prominent trustee, called the leaders of the dissatisfied group a "Scotch Club," given, so they said, to plotting against the trustees' representatives, living wastefully and wantonly, with "an imperios manner of behaviour." Thomas Causton, first bailiff of Savannah and storekeeper employed by the trustees, reported that ill feeling between the Scotch group and others was so intense that a millwright worker, having taken more than his share of spirits, threatened two stalwarts of the Scotch Club "& swore if he could have his will, he would knock them Scotch Sons of Bitches brains out." A delegation from the "Club" visited Causton after this incident and complained heatedly, but received little satisfaction. Others, especially Thomas Jones, offered a more sweeping indictment against the group: dressing gaily; setting up a Free masons club, a St. Andrews club and "other Tipling Societies"; keeping concubines; and holding horse races for pleasure at a time when the colony was in danger of an invasion from the Spanish.[36]

Although the Scotch Club and other dissatisfied elements obviously were not responsible for Georgia's troubles as some contemporaries erroneously believed, it is equally apparent that the problems that arose in the colony presented the leaders of the movement with an opportunity to seek their own ends: first, to force concessions from the trustees that would enable the planter who wished to carry on commercial agriculture to use greater discretion in exploiting his holdings; and second, to assure the planter and his associates of extensive policy-making power over the affairs of the province, a political objective. It is possible and, in fact, highly probable that the leaders of the malcontents did not have these goals clearly in mind initially, but there can be no question about their intentions by 1741. They wished to alter fundamentally the character of the colony, to refashion it in the image of other English settlements with control firmly retained by themselves. The demand that originated with a specific adjustment of policy concluded on a note that nothing less than the principle of liberty was at issue.

Individual grievances had been presented to the trustees since the founding of the colony, but formal evidence of deep-seated discontent did not appear until 9 December 1738, when approximately 130 prominent settlers, largely from Savannah, signed a memorial protesting against the management of the colony. William Stephens asserted that Robert Williams and Patrick Tailfer were the "chief fabricators," but it would be a mistake to think that the memorial was the product of an inconsequential minority.[37] Considering that it was signed only by men, it represented perhaps as many as five hundred colonists, a substantial number from the infant settlement.[38] Moreover, it was signed despite a warning from the officials of the trustees not to participate in the memorial. When it is recalled that these officials had absolute control of the colony's affairs, it is surprising that anyone signed.

The memorial of 1738 is not an impassioned document but a remarkably able, logical disquisition—from a distinct point of view. It included a discriminating description of the progress of the Georgia settlement and its problems, stressing the limitations of the soil and the absence of a staple for export. Each year, the memorial argued, a planter loses money, thereby reducing him to bankruptcy. Without a staple for export there could be no market, no trade, and no prosperity. Using lumber products as an example, the memorialists complained that it was difficult to compete with the cheaper slave labor of South Carolina, adding that their inability to obtain credit seriously hampered the colony's economy. So far as the money provided by Parliament and dispensed by the trustees was concerned, it had been used primarily for defense. And what would bring about a solution, asked the memorialists? Land tenures should be modified, giving the landowners titles in fee simple, and permission should be given to import a limited number of black slaves.

Many of the problems described were genuine enough, but it is difficult to see how the changes suggested would have quickly disposed of them. As later generations were to learn, what could be grown in Virginia or the Carolinas could not necessarily be produced profitably in Georgia. The memorialists, in advocating limited slavery and a change of land tenure, were unquestionably led to the conclusion that the relative prosperity of the remaining southern colonies as opposed to their distressing conditions must be attributable to the most obvious dissimilarities, a distinctive labor force and land system.

When the trustees learned of the memorial in April 1739, they remained unmoved by the request for limited slavery, and they hesitated to act on the issue of land tenure. But, more important, they tended to minimize the depressed circumstances prevailing within the colony, to dismiss the discontent as inspired by men of limited vision who were guided only by self-interest, and to magnify the accomplishments of the colony and its immediate prospects.

The trustees replied with some heat that they "should deem them Selves very unfit for the Trust reposed in them by his Majesty on their behalf if they could be prevailed upon, by such an irrational Attempt, to give up a Constitution framed with the greatest Caution for the Preservation of Liberty and Property; and of which the Laws against the Use of slaves, and for the Entail of Lands are the Surest Foundation[.]" Under the present system, they declared, property was protected. If modifications were permitted, all property would soon be in the hands of the Negro merchants. In short, the trustees placed little confidence in the accepted concept of property rights as generally, if not universally, accepted by Englishmen in the eighteenth century.[39]

Despite the obvious sincerity and good intentions on the part of the trustees, no attitude, in fact, could have been better calculated to provoke animosity among those who signed the memorial than a complacent reply. It could only result in more strenuous efforts to break through the ring of self-satisfaction, the acceptance of things as they were, efforts that by their very nature would be less moderate in tone, less concerned with good faith and reasonableness.

This mood of restlessness and frustration on the part of the memorialists was intensified by the actions of the supporters and representatives of the trustees in the colony. In October 1739 Governor Oglethorpe himself sent a long message to the trustees under the general title of the "State of Georgia," defending the policies that had operated in the colony since its founding. And on 19 November 1739, William Stephens, secretary to the colony, called a meeting of the inhabitants of Savannah, placed a memorial before them entitled "A State of the Province of Georgia" which noted the colony's accomplishments and flourishing condition, and asked them to sign it. It is instructive to compare the similarity between many parts of "A State of the Province of Georgia" and Oglethorpe's original "State of Georgia." It becomes evident that the Savannah inhabitants were being asked to sign a statement, prepared in substantial part by Oglethorpe, giving Oglethorpe's and the trustees' view of the condition of the colony. Yet the document was to be forwarded as representing the views and opinions of the settlers. Pressure from local spokesmen for the trustees did not prevail, and only twenty-odd inhabitants signed the document.[40]

In another effort to counter the memorials of the discontented, Oglethorpe organized petitions among the Scotch Highlanders and Salzburgers, reaffirming the importance of the trustees' policy to prohibit the importation of black slaves. Interestingly, about the same time the Highlanders received additional cattle bought at Oglethorpe's order, and the Salzburgers reported that Oglethorpe had promised assistance in getting more of their like-minded Lutherans transported to Georgia.

These countermoves did not halt the developing crisis. Not only was a remonstrance forwarded to the trustees by the dissatisfied colonists, enlarging upon their earlier complaints, but also the group drew up a petition, dated a month later and thus before the remonstrance could be acted upon, to carry their case directly to the Crown and Parliament. To familiar demands, modification of land titles and the limited importation of slaves, new demands were added: land should be granted where it was convenient for settlers, excessive quitrents should be eased and their imposition delayed, and a voice be given the settlers in choosing colonial magistrates. Complaining that the trustees regarded the request of Georgia as coming from a "Set of Clamourous people, Influenced by designing men and Negroe Merchants," the petitioners asserted that their sole objective was to alleviate the conditions within the colony, appealing, significantly, to "ye [the] famous Declaration of Rights made by our Fore Fathers at ye [the] Glorious Revolution[.]" [41]

Indeed, it was the theme of rightful liberty that began to assert itself in the petitions of 1740–1741. It was thought in the "nature of Britons" to establish their own system of local magistrates. The management of the colony's affairs as it was now operating was contrary to the Declaration of Rights, an elemental document defining British liberty in the eighteenth century. Unless the colony's affairs were altered, "a number of Members of the Common wealth, that with Lawfull liberty might be usefull in the Society, will sink into destruction and ruin." [42]

John Fallowfield, appointed bailiff by the trustees because he was admired for his industry, loyalty, and intelligence, reported in the same tenor, thoroughly critical of the trustees' representatives in Georgia. The province "Groans under the insupportable Tyranny" of some people here who operate under the authority of the trustees, he wrote. "Their [the Georgia settlers] naturall Rights are denied them, the priviledges of British Subjects are withheld from them, The protection of the Laws of the Nation, whereof they are members if [are] refused them." Fallowfield particularly identified Thomas Jones as the chief actor in "Dispotick Measures." When Fallowfield was sharply criticized by the trustees because of his letter, he boldly retorted, "Your honours say persons not content with Government are equally unable to Govern themselves, we are able to Govern our selves, and think you unable to chuse Governors for us, as we best know the people, and who is fittest for the Magistracy," phrasing that reminds the reader of Tom Paine's *Common Sense*, which was not to appear for more than three decades.[43] What had obviously begun as a challenge to the policies of the trustees had now turned into a question of principle: Who has the right to govern?

V

With the dispatch of the remonstrance to the king and Parliament, events now began to take shape for the publication of *A True and Historical Narrative*, the composition that brought the Georgia issue to a climax. The background of this extraordinary document, written by Patrick Tailfer, a physician, Hugh Anderson, a well-educated gentleman, and David Douglas, all former residents of Georgia now living in South Carolina, has been explored elsewhere. Suffice it to say that it demolished the image of Oglethorpe, swept aside trustee claims of Georgia's potential success as a colony, detailed every shortcoming of the colony, provoked an outpouring of pamphlets authorized by the trustees rebutting the claims of the *Narrative*, and crystallized the case against further subsidies to Georgia by Parliament. Although the authors of the *Narrative* overstated the case, the true conditions in Georgia were revealed. It was only a matter of time before the Crown would regain control of the colony, which it did in June 1752. By that date land policies had been drastically altered and ownership of slaves on a limited scale had begun.[44]

But the trusteeship period in Georgia history left a legacy that enriched the southern mosaic, not to mention writing a unique chapter in the history of the British colonies in North America. The absence of genuine colonial and local government in Georgia meant that social obligations such as the care of the poor and orphans, colonial defense, and a host of other human problems were not resolved in the same ways as in other colonies. The establishment of an orphans' house by the Salzburgers and the creation of the celebrated orphans' house of Whitefield on a grander scale became Georgia's answer to social responsibilities that county courts resolved in North Carolina and Virginia or that parishes accepted in South Carolina. (It is scarcely an accident that similar projects for orphans failed to develop in other colonies.) These governmental institutions did not exist in trusteeship Georgia, so the solution to social problems became a private rather than a public responsibility, privately rather than publicly funded. The trustees' store served as the vehicle to care for the indigent, only in the case of Georgia the percentage of inhabitants who were eventually included in this category constituted perhaps the majority of the settlers. When Georgia did become a royal colony, the development of county government lagged.

The need for local defense in other British colonies in North America rested exclusively on the settlers. In the case of Georgia, although it had been planned so that each grantee held a military fief and everyone would fly to the call of arms when danger threatened, the burden of defense fell, ironically, upon the mother country, which supplied a permanent contingent of British Rangers. In some ways, especially in southern Georgia, the colony became a military settlement.

Encouraging a variety of peoples from widely separated backgrounds and holding dissimilar beliefs—how strikingly the Georgia "model" differs from that of Massachusetts Bay—gave Georgia a rich ethnic diversity that it never lost. Indeed, trustee policies, regardless of the controversy over why they were adopted, attempted to develop a slaveless society, and, somewhat less well understood, a womanless society because of its land policies. Outside of New Ebenezer, the Salzburger settlement, demographic estimates confirm this conclusion. The imbalance in the ratio between men and women appears to have been carried beyond the years of the American Revolution, making the social composition of Georgia distinctive from its colonial counterparts, another aspect of the texture of the mosaic reflected in the southern colonies.

FOUR

Slaves, Slavery, and the Genesis of the Plantation System in South Carolina:

An Evolving Social-Economic Mosaic

HOW OFTEN DO SCHOLARS NOTE THAT THE SOCIAL-ECONOMIC origin of South Carolina is unique, for it is the only English colony in North America in which black slavery is introduced almost at the outset of settlement and certainly by 1671![1]

Historians, professional and popular, have been studying or writing about slaves, slavery, and the plantation system for two centuries or more, and recent scholarly investigations have focused on racial attitudes, their origins and consequences. Yet historians know little about slaves or slavery in the eighteenth-century southern colonies. Ignorance of this important subject is not likely to be dispelled soon. No apology is needed, therefore, for attempting to illuminate the origins of slavery and the emergence of the plantation system in South Carolina as a case study that enriches an understanding of the social-economic mosaic in the southern colonies.[2]

I

There are two vexing problems confronting scholars when investigating slaves, slavery, and the plantation system of

South Carolina. The first is the absence of internal records. For the early period, 1670–1730, there are no diaries, no newspapers, and, at best, only fugitive items of internal communication. Neither a group of plantation records nor the ongoing record of a single plantation exists for the colonial period. To discover what is happening to the colony's economy or social system, the scholar must make imaginative use of external evidence.

The second serious problem involves an extended list of assumptions historians traditionally tend to make about colonial South Carolina: that the introduction of slavery as a labor force was somehow preordained because of the staples produced, especially in a semitropical climate; that the Africans who arrived were ignorant and incompetent; that from the beginning white Carolinians regarded the African as inferior and incapable; that slavery and the plantation system developed simultaneously and, as a corollary, that the growth of slavery corresponded with the expansion of rice plantations; and finally, that slavery, once introduced into South Carolina, generally followed the frontier line during the colonial period, resulting in a relatively uniform social composition of whites and blacks throughout the colony with all the consequences as they relate to economic and political interests.

Without responding to each supposition, either in the order named or at equal length, it is imperative that fact be distinguished from loose or undocumented generalizations. On the issue of how, when, and why slavery expanded and the plantation system emerged, this essay will demonstrate that the assertions of previous historians have been in error.

With the perspective offered by modern scholarship, it is now possible to agree that the Africans brought to America came as immigrants, forcibly transported, and that for historians to understand them, they must be studied in the same context as peoples who came from Europe, Asia, or

any other land. Africans brought their culture with them—
their values, beliefs, traditions, and skills. Modern historians
of Africa have demonstrated beyond dispute that the peoples
of West and East Africa were gifted tropical farmers. They
knew how to herd cattle, to tend rice fields, to raise grain,
and to use agricultural implements. Indeed, Africans were
often more familiar with the requisite farming techniques
than the settlers who came from England or Europe.

There is also sufficient evidence to question whether the
attitude of white settlers in South Carolina toward Africans
was as fixed as recent writers have claimed, in particular,
whether whites considered the blacks as inferior. From the
earliest settlement until the conclusion of the Yamasee War
in 1718, a period of almost fifty years, blacks were entrusted
with responsibilities for defense that almost equalled those
of whites. Moreover, there is positive proof that blacks were
considered fully competent to serve in the militia as armed
men equipped to fight. In a pamphlet published in 1710,
promoting South Carolina, for which Thomas Nairne, the
celebrated Carolina Indian agent, is believed to have supplied the authoritative and reliable information, the following observation is made: "There are likewise enrolled
in our Militia, a considerable Number of active, able, Negro Slaves; and the Law gives everyone of those his Freedom, who in the Time of an Invasion kills an Enemey." [3]

An item on Charleston dated 27 April 1708, included in
The Boston News-Letter of 17–24 May 1708, reinforces
the assertion of Thomas Nairne:

Charlstown, South-Carolina, April 27. By Letters from
Jamaica we are informed, that the *French* and *Spaniards* are
raising a Force of 2500 men, and 'tis supposed they have a
design to make a second attempt upon this Province; that
which gives some umbrage to it is, some persons lately taken
from St. *Augustin,* who say, that a Brigt. and Sloop were arrived there from the *Havanna,* which caused great accla-

mations of joy amongst the *Spaniards*. This Intelligence
has caused an Embargo to be continued, and we are making all necessary preparations of Fortifying and Entrench-
ing, to give the Enemy a warm reception; we shall have
1500 white men well arm'd, 1000 good Negroes that knows
the Swamps and Woods, most of them Cattle-hunters, besides 1500 Indians.[4]

In the Yamasee War of 1715–1718 blacks were used not as
auxiliaries but as front-line troops. The defense line in 1715
as reported by Governor Charles Craven was composed of
six hundred Carolina militia, one hundred men from Virginia and North Carolina, and four to five hundred slaves
and Indians. "I have caused about two hundred stout negro
men to be enlisted," he wrote, "and these with a party of
white men and Indians are marching towards the enemy."
The following year the Carolina proprietors reported to the
Board of Trade: "They [South Carolina] will be able upon
any great Emergency to arm their Negroes and by these
means they will be Impowered to resist a greater Force than
the Indian Enemy will in all humane [human] probability
be able at any time to bring against them." [5]

A fascinating sidelight in recruiting manpower to fight
the Yamasee War is that Virginia, slow to honor its pledge
to aid South Carolina, demanded that one female slave be
sent to Virginia for every able-bodied man sent to reinforce
the fighting force in Carolina. Not only did Carolinians
complain of the limited numbers and the quality of the
Virginians who arrived, but they also refused to send female
slaves as requested, "finding it impracticable to Send Negro
Women in their Roomes by reason of the Discontent such
Usage would have given their husbands to have their wives
taken from them which might have occasioned a Revolt." [6]

It would be foolish to claim too much for this evidence on
white attitudes toward blacks, but the extant contemporary
comments do not suggest that blacks were considered incom-

petent, inferior, or "less than men." It should also be noted
that evidence advanced to support a contrary position in
white attitudes during this early period is equally fragmentary. One generalization about white attitudes toward
blacks in the colony is conclusive. After the celebrated
Stono Rebellion of 1739, white Carolinians lived in desperate fear of blacks and slave uprisings, a state of mind affecting every aspect of the black and white relationship.

On the question of territorial containment of slavery in
South Carolina, that seldom read but pioneering scholar,
Robert L. Meriwether, proved over three decades ago that
the plantation system based on slavery was confined to the
coastal region during the entire colonial period. The South
Carolina Township System, introduced in the late 1720s
and executed in the subsequent decades, set a firm bound-
ary surrounding the low country plantations. It established, as a deliberate policy, a broad band of buffer settlements, frequently composed of non-English groups from
Western Europe, in which the demographic ratio of whites
to blacks was overwhelmingly white. The township system
effectively fulfilled the expectations of those who planned
it. As a result, plantation slavery did not penetrate the up-
country until cotton became a profitable enterprise after
the American Revolution.[7]

II

The genesis of the plantation system and its relationship to
the growth of slavery in South Carolina has been seriously
misread by scholars, in large measure because the history of
the colony has been perceived from the American Revolution to its origins rather than from the initial settlement to
the 1720s. The mistaken but unchallenged generalization
accepts as fact that an increase in rice production with its
demand for a substantial labor force, was responsible for the

rapid increase of slaves and, as a parallel, the evolution of the plantation system. The fallacy of this assumption can be proven only by an analysis of the development of the Carolina economy in relation to the composition and disposition of its labor force between 1690 and 1720.

In 1690 the exports of the colony of South Carolina were negligible. Rice cultivation lay in the future, as did the development of naval stores. Only the products of ranch farming—beef and pork, pease and grain—and trade in deerskins found an outside market. Although estimates indicate that as much as half the population was composed of blacks, and almost all of them slaves, the plantation system, as historians conceive it, did not exist. The colony, therefore, represented a rare species among the British colonies in North America, having a predominately black slave labor force without the production of a significant agricultural staple for export.

The presence of such a large proportion of blacks in relationship to the total population without an overwhelming demand for their labor appears to be almost accidental. In the process of migrating to South Carolina, individual Barbadians transported a few slaves. Although the total number was relatively modest, the scarcity of white colonizers automatically heightened the percentage of blacks.[8]

However fragmentary the record, there is no reliable evidence to suggest that from the earliest settlement to 1690 black slaves were imported separately as distinct from being part of the white migration which owned servants and slaves. As late as the first half-decade after 1700, annual slave importations failed to reach twenty-five, a figure apparently greatly exceeded by the export of Indian slaves, mostly to the West Indies and New England, not to mention their employment in Carolina where it is estimated they comprised one fourth of the slave labor force as late as 1708. It can be inferred, in the absence of evidence to the contrary, that the number of blacks in South Carolina in the 1690s was principally the result of natural increase.[9]

As to the export of Indian slaves, the records are not sufficiently consistent or complete to present them graphically, but as late as the year 1712–1713 no less than seventy-five Indian slaves were shipped out of Charleston. Even though the capture of Indians caused ill will and often encouraged warfare between tribes—which scarcely served the ends of the deerskin trade because warriors do not have time to hunt—a rationale, involving convoluted and misconceived concepts of humanity, is offered in a memorial written by Thomas Nairne, dated 10 July 1709: "Some men think that it both serves to lessen their [the Indian] numbers before the French can arm them, and it is a more effectuall way of civilising and instructing [them], then all the efforts used by the French missionaries." [10]

Given the unusual situation governing black and Indian slaves about 1690, an assessment of the significance of the deerskin trade during the early stages of South Carolina's economic development is particularly enlightening. The Indian trade was the swiftest way to achieve success, yet virtually no slave labor was needed for it to flourish. In 1705 Nairne, who served as the Commons House of Assembly's first official representative in Indian country, described the trade as "the main Branch of . . . Traffick," meaning the most lucrative commercial activity, because, in absolute numbers, far more people were engaged in ranch farming. John Lawson, a contemporary frontiersman, reinforced Nairne's conclusion when he observed that those men engaged in the Indian trade had "soonest rais'd themselves of any People I have known in Carolina." [11]

As Figure 1 indicates, the number of deerskins shipped out from Charleston between 1698 and 1723—only in the northern colonies was fur an important article of Indian trade—fluctuated widely. In 1699, 64,000 deerskins were exported, but the following year this figure was reduced almost two thirds to 22,000. In 1707, with the domestic turmoil of the Church Establishment issue settled and the Indian Trade Act adopted, 121,000 deerskins were shipped, a number not equalled for several decades. In dramatic contrast, in 1716 during the Yamasee War only 4,000 skins were sent to market. This erratic behavior in the pattern of the export of deerskins did not arise from changing competitive conditions but because of Indian wars, internal policies affecting the trade and similar disruptions.

Although the quantities of deerskins exported are known, their value is not. Commodity price lists are not available until the 1730s, so estimates can be made only by indirection. Between 1708 and 1715 the average number of deerskins exported was approximately 50,000. During this same period, the value of all exports to Great Britain—which served as the principal market for deerskins—averaged, according to British customs records, about 23,000 pounds sterling. In 1717 the Carolina Commissioners of the Indian Trade offered 2 shillings 6 pence, apparently sterling, or its equivalent in goods, for each deerskin. Taking this figure as an approximation, the average value of the export of deerskins amounted to one fourth the value of the total exports to Britain. But this percentage would seem to understate seriously the importance of the trade in deerskins not only as an export but also as a source of funds to build a fortune. For example, as late as 1750 a report by Governor James Glen stated that deerskins constituted 20 percent of the value of all exports to Britain. Certainly in the period 1690–1710 deerskins must have contributed up to one half the value of exports to Britain. The answer to the discrepancy between 25 percent or 50 percent of the value of exports probably lies in transportation costs and other charges incurred in bringing deerskins to market. These costs must

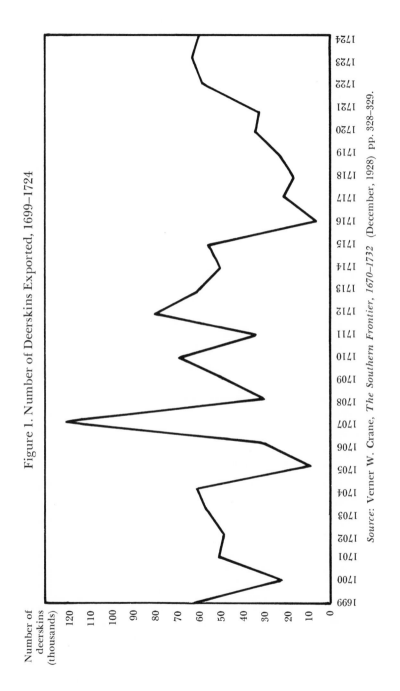

Figure 1. Number of Deerskins Exported, 1699–1724

Number of deerskins (thousands)

Source: Verner W. Crane, *The Southern Frontier, 1670–1732* (December, 1928) pp. 328–329.

be added to the Carolina price to obtain a figure equivalent in kind to the customs values given in England.

A final indicator of the role of the Indian trade in the economic activity of South Carolina was the value of the importation of trading goods from Britain. Verner Crane, the outstanding authority, quotes a contemporary to the effect that the value of such goods by 1715 was 10,000 pounds sterling annually. The evidence suggests that this figure is overstated. The value of all British exports to South Carolina in 1715, according to official records, was 16,000 pounds sterling, and in no previous year had the value exceeded 28,000 pounds sterling. Over the period preceding 1715 it averaged less than 20,000 pounds sterling. That one half of all exports from Britain were Indian trading goods is questionable. If accurate, the figure exceeds by 100 percent the value of deerskins as exports. Even if the approximation of the value of the deerskins exported is in error by 100 percent, the importation of trading goods would merely equal the value of deerskins exported. This, too, seems highly unlikely.[12]

As the earliest staple commodity to emerge in the South Carolina economy, the deerskin trade contributed to capital accumulation, providing one means of obtaining money and credit to buy land and slaves. But the evidence is not available to establish such a correlation. What records exist do not indicate either that an increase in the number of slaves coincides with the prosperity of the Indian trade or that the number of slaves relates to the fluctuations of the trade. It is possible that over a period of decades individuals engaged in the Indian trade enlarged their slave holdings, but this assertion must be regarded as speculative rather than factual.

Certainly, the deerskin trade strengthened the role of Charleston as a commercial port, because it became the terminus for a web of trails winding thousands of miles into

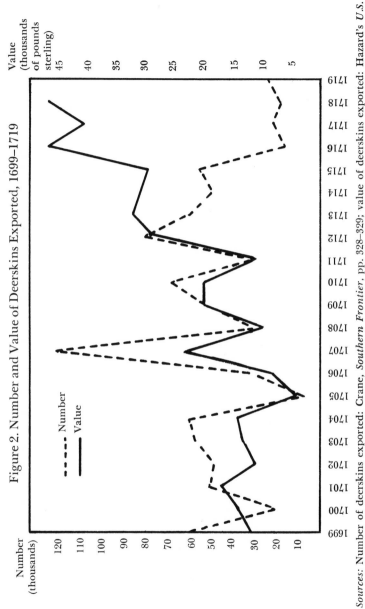

Figure 2. Number and Value of Deerskins Exported, 1699–1719

Number (thousands)

Value (thousands of pounds sterling)

Number

Value

Sources: Number of deerskins exported: Crane, Southern Frontier, pp. 328–329; value of deerskins exported: Hazard's U.S. Commercial and Statistical Register (Philadelphia, 1840), p. 4.

the Indian country. Charleston also became more colorful as rough-and-ready traders from the frontier—"Those sparkes make little of drinking 15 or 16£ at one Bout in Towne"—jostled shoulders with those settlers engaged in more traditional occupations. Occasionally an important Indian chief accompanied by his retinue and decked out in ceremonial dress added to the tableau.[13]

The full importance of the Indian trade can be understood only in the perspective of international rivalries, domestic politics, and finally the close relationship of Carolina's exports of deerskins to the total value of the trade to Great Britain until 1712, as represented in Figure 2. Indeed, 1712 is a key year, and the period from 1710 to 1720 is a critical decade in an analysis of how and why plantation slavery suddenly flourished in South Carolina.

III

Ranch farming offered the first opportunity to make effective use of a slave labor force. Blacks became cowboys in proprietary South Carolina long before they appeared on the Great Plains in the nineteenth century. Until the emergence of commercial ranch farming, a labor supply was in search of an agricultural staple, a dramatic contrast to the customary condition in most English colonies in North America in which the development of an agricultural staple became the first step in an increased demand for a labor supply.

As early as 1682 Samuel Wilson reported that "Neat Cattle thrive and increase here exceedingly, there being perticular Planters that have already seven or eight hundred head." Almost thirty years later, *A Letter From South Carolina* (1710) reconfirmed that observation. "South Carolina abounds with black Cattle to a Degree much beyond any other English colony." Samuel Wilson also indicated that the feeding of hogs flourished, bringing in sufficient profit to encourage the purchase of servants and black slaves. "That there are many Planters that are single and have never a Servant, that have two or three hundred Hogs, of which they make great profit; Barbados, Jamaica, and New-England, affording a constant good price for their Pork; by which means they get wherewithal to build them more convenient Houses, and to purchase Servants, and Negro-slaves." [14]

Conditions favored raising livestock. Comparatively speaking, in producing a marketable agricultural staple, ranch farming required a minimum investment in capital and labor. Moreover, many Barbadians who migrated to South Carolina were experienced in this type of farming. The mild climate of the colony also reduced the need to store fodder and construct shelters, important considerations in employing a labor force most efficiently. Herding cattle also tended to be less seasonal than other types of farming. Although ranch farming was practiced throughout proprietary South Carolina, its stronghold was in Colleton County, southeast of Charleston, and the slender evidence available seems to indicate that the flow of black labor was toward that region.

Production of livestock quickly outstripped local consumption, and beef and pork became one of Carolina's earliest exports. The best evidence of this trade is an enactment of 1691, later invalidated by the proprietors, which attempted to introduce a degree of regulation. After declaring that "beefe and porke are two of the principal commodities" of this part of the province, the act proceeded to specify the type and size of barrel that were to be used in packing and how the barrels should be marked. It provided for an inspection system with penalties for "deceits" where "bull's flesh, boare's flesh, or any other unmerchantable or corrupt meate" was mixed with good beef or pork. No unmarked barrel was to be permitted on shipboard. This law, reenacted later, indicates how well developed the trade in meat products had become.[15]

These provisions were marketed primarily in the West Indies. The evidence as to the specific quantity and value of beef and pork is sparse. A report presented in England to illustrate the importance of South Carolina to the mother country listed among the exports of Charleston from June 1712 to June 1713 beef in the amount of 1,963 barrels and pork in the amount of 1,241 barrels.[16]

In 1715 the disruptive Yamasee War wiped out the ranchers. Their territorial expansion southeast of Charleston represented a direct threat to the Indians. Ranches were overrun and buildings and possessions burned. Crops were destroyed in the fields, and the livestock taken or slaughtered. Contemporaries estimated that in 1716 alone one half the land being farmed was of necessity abandoned. Until the 1730s, when ranch farming reappeared in a different location and under different conditions, it never fully recovered from this destruction.[17]

Ranch farming, much like the Indian trade, placed its stamp upon proprietary South Carolina. Problems arose resembling those of the cattle frontier in the second half of the nineteenth century. Identifying marks and brands were used, and registration of the brands was required by law. Unmarked livestock could not be slaughtered—obviously because such license would open the way to poaching and fraud—until ownership was determined. Early in the eighteenth century Carolina had its roundups in which cattle were driven into a cowpen, usually a wooden pen constructed by the planter or a location where two streams converged. Fencing, the transfer of ownership of livestock, and the problems identified with ranch farming became part of a familiar pattern in the everyday life of most settlers.

IV

Between 1710 and 1715 the economy of South Carolina changed fundamentally. The dimension of this transformation is best revealed in the available export figures. They can be succinctly summarized as follows:

First, during this period the correlation between the volume of the deerskin trade and the value of exports to Britain ends, the curve of the former descending precipitously and that of the latter sweeping upward. From this evidence a scholar must conclude that the deerskin trade, although it continues to be significant, has been superseded in importance by other staples for export.

Second, simultaneously, the export of provisions achieved its zenith, declining abruptly in 1715 with the wholesale destruction of the assets of ranch farmers by hostile Indians at the outbreak of the Yamasee War. The decline in beef and pork exports continued for several decades.

Third, between 1700 and 1712 the production of rice increased swiftly, but after 1712 it gradually declined and then held steady until 1720.

And finally, from 1710 to 1720 the manufacture of naval stores rose sharply, coinciding with two other crucial developments, the incremental rise of the value of exports to Britain from 17,000 pounds sterling in 1713 to an excess of 60,000 pounds sterling in 1720, an expansion of 250 percent, and a dramatic augmentation in the importation of black slaves, from less than 100 annually in 1712 to 600 annually in 1720. Of these striking alterations, the last two developments require an exploration in depth in order to provide the background as to how, when, and why the South Carolina plantation system emerged.

The story of the introduction of rice into Carolina by a ship's captain from Madagascar who touched in at Charles-

ton in 1694 because his ship was in danger of sinking, thus
providing a small bag of that commodity to a prominent
planter, has long since been revised by the findings of scholars. Experimentation with rice cultivation along with silk
and cotton had been attempted early in the colony's history,
but it was not an immediate success. Rude conditions in the
early years of settlement discouraged the type of intensive
agriculture which rice growing represented at the same time
encouraging ranch farming and the trade in deerskins in
which manpower problems were minimized and where the
market was assured. Confidence in an attractive financial
return for other commodities tended to preclude any large-
scale shift to planting rice.

Producing rice for market began in the middle 1690s,
yet it only reached an export level of 2,000 barrels by 1700.
According to the most reliable figures available, between
June 1712 and June 1713 the export of rice was 12,677 barrels and 200 bags, an increase of 600 percent over 1700. At
this stage in the analysis, its cultivation would appear to be
the vital ingredient in explaining an emerging plantation
system and the growth of slavery.[18]

But suddenly and surprisingly rice exports declined after
1712–1713, a fact historians have tended to obscure. Exports
fell immediately from about 12,000 to 9,000 barrels, 25 percent, and then leveled off for the remainder of the decade,
when a contemporary observer reported that a fresh spurt
raised exports to 13,000 barrels. The behavior of rice production from 1710 to 1720 reveals that it bore little relationship to slave importation between 1695 and 1713 and
none after 1713.[19]

Cultivation of rice began to flourish in South Carolina in
the moist, almost swampy lowland country, adjacent to
freshwater streams and rivulets that periodically overflowed.
These requisite soil properties ultimately—but not as early
as 1713—placed a natural limit upon the territorial expan-

sion of rice production. In 1706 and again in 1707, 24 and
22 slaves, respectively, were imported during those years,
no doubt some of them being purchased by rice planters. A
Report to the Board of Trade in 1708–1709 suggests that
approximately 500 Negro slaves, 300 males and 200 females,
were brought to Charleston during the previous five years.
The same report indicates a substantial percentage of the
labor force was made up of Indian slaves. From 1708 to
1711 the number of slave importations increased markedly,
from 53 for 1708 to 170 for 1711, and then declined abruptly to about 75 in 1712. (See Figure 5.) Unquestionably,
some of these slaves did serve as the labor force in rice fields,
but, strangely, there is no contemporary evidence to indicate that large numbers were imported for the production
of rice as a deliberate policy, a contrast to the conscious effort to bring in slaves to expand the manufacture of naval
stores beginning in 1713.

The value of 10,000 barrels of rice exported, compared
with other staples marketed, is difficult to determine. No
price schedule exists. Those provided by a buyer at a given
time and place cannot be checked to ascertain whether they
are representative. On the premise that the prices of 1710
are the equal of those about 1720, 2 shillings per hundred
weight, the value of rice exports would be approximately
10,000 pounds sterling annually from 1710 to 1720.

Why rice production failed to increase from 1713 to 1720
is not easily explained. The effect of British regulation,
though profound, was a constant factor. In 1690 Parliament
laid a tax on rice of approximately 3 pence a pound sterling.
Two years later an ad valorem duty of 5 percent was added.
In 1705 rice was placed on the enumerated list, which meant
that it must, like tobacco, be sent first to England before it
could, after paying the appropriate custom duties, be re-
exported. The duties were burdensome and the enumera-
tion a serious handicap because the Iberian peninsula rep-

resented a principal market. Despite these handicaps, against which the colonials protested vigorously, rice output increased until 1712 when, inexplicably, it declined. Perhaps instability on the frontier inhibited opening additional land for cultivation or the price of rice fell, a theory that cannot be verified. Certainly, for a few years the Yamasee War ended almost all production, but by that date rice exports had already declined.

V

The final step in the transformation of the economy of South Carolina took place between 1712 and 1720. The key ingredient was the development of naval stores which formed the base for a full-fledged plantation system based on slave labor. Again, the export-import figures serve as the indicators of this profound internal change. These statistics indicate (1) the sudden spurt in the value of exports to Britain during this period coincides with the acceleration in the manufacture of naval stores; (2) the rise in marketing naval stores marks an abrupt departure in the relationship between the value of exports to, as compared with the value of imports from, Britain; (3) the rapid expansion in the importation of slaves, more than 300 percent, correlates with the increasing exports of naval stores and signals the flowering of the plantation system based on slave labor. Furthermore, naval stores acted as the catalyst which, in the second decade of the eighteenth century, brought prosperity to the white population of South Carolina and converted a fundamentally subsistence economy to one of boundless commercial growth.

The relationship of the development of naval stores to the economy of South Carolina and especially to the emerging plantation system has seldom been fully appreciated. As early as 1699 Surveyor General Edward Randolph, after visiting the colony, recommended that soldiers be dispatched to protect its exposed frontier, asserting that the troops could readily maintain themselves by planting Indian corn and by making pitch and tar as a marketable product. He also observed that the basis of Carolina's economic strength was "Pitch, Tar and Turpentine, and planting rice," a coupling of equals which historians have not always recognized.[20]

The production and export of naval stores from South Carolina expanded rapidly after 1705 when Great Britain, eager to limit its dependence upon the Baltic countries for these indispensable goods and disturbed over a sharp rise in prices, offered a bounty of 4 pounds sterling per ton for pitch (each ton to contain 20 gross hundreds in 8 barrels), 4 pounds sterling per ton for tar (each ton to contain 8 barrels of 31½ gallons each), and 3 pounds sterling per ton for turpentine (20 gross hundreds in 8 barrels). In the following decade further encouragement was provided by appointing a "surveyor of woods" who was to instruct the colonists in the best methods of manufacturing naval stores and the establishment of a fund to employ skilled workmen and to supply tools for this purpose.[21]

The appointment of a surveyor of woods was prompted by the criticism leveled against the quality of naval stores from Carolina. Its products, it was asserted, did not compare favorably with those from the Baltic countries, especially in pitch and tar, which retained, as described by one observer, a "heating" quality. This complication developed apparently because Carolina settlers used dead rather than live trees in making pitch and tar. Francis Yonge, a contemporary who appraised the problem, declared that no one could recognize the appropriate pitch or lightwood pine in a forest of timber. As many as twenty trees, he continued, would have to be cut down before one or two could be found worth putting into a kiln. Such waste of manpower in a region where labor needed to be employed most effectively was, of course, considered intolerable. Moreover, a green pine tree yielded only one third that of "old wood," again adding to the costs. In view of these factors, it is not surprising that the Carolina settlers continued to follow their own methods.[22]

It is possible that the complaint about the character of South Carolina pitch and tar was overdrawn. In 1717, when productivity in South Carolina was booming, the Board of Trade was informed not only that the Carolina products were widely used but also that no objections were raised as to their quality.

Whether or not the criticism of South Carolina naval stores was valid has no bearing upon the startling growth of naval stores and its significance in the emergence of the plantation system in South Carolina. Although few reliable estimates exist for the earliest years, 2,037 barrels of tar and 4,580 barrels of pitch, a total of 6,617 barrels, were exported from South Carolina between June 1712 and June 1713.[23] By 1717 the export of tar amounted to 29,594 barrels, that of pitch 14,363, a total of 43,957 barrels. In 1718–1719 the export of tar was 32,117, that of pitch 20,208, a total of 52,215. These figures represent an increase between 1712 and 1719 in excess of 800 percent.[24]

This upward thrust in the commercial life of the colony induced by the development of naval stores corresponds with the steeply inclined curve measuring the value of imports from South Carolina to Britain (see Figure 3). Between 1712 and 1719 the total export of Carolina to Britain, in terms of value, increased from 29,000 pounds sterling to 50,000 pounds sterling. This statistic minimizes rather than maximizes the trend. If the range of years is extended from 1711 to 1720, the value of exports to Britain grew from 11,000 pounds sterling to 60,000 pounds sterling. Although the 1711 figure is slightly out of line on the downside, the

Value
(thousands
of pounds
sterling)

Figure 3. Value of South Carolina Exports and Imports, 1697–1730

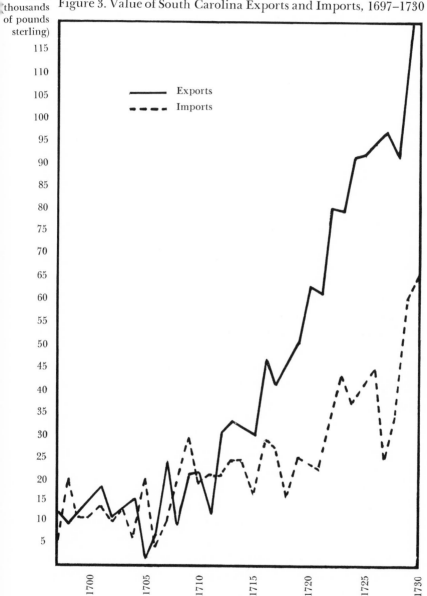

1720 figure properly reflects the swiftly ascending curve measuring the value of exports. In view of the constant or declining export of rice and deerskins, only the acceleration in the rise of naval stores can account for this rapid increase in the value of exports.

Considered as part of the total inflow of naval stores into Britain from 1711 to 1718, the contribution made by South Carolina is striking. In 1712, according to Board of Trade statistics, 5,624 barrels of pitch and tar were imported from all the colonies and the following year 4,825. Exports of pitch and tar from Charleston alone, during the period June 1712 to June 1713, was 6,617 barrels, which suggests that Carolina could produce the total amount imported into England from all its colonies and still export a quantity to other markets.

From 1715 to 1718 British imports of pitch and tar from its colonies rose from 5,000 barrels to 82,000 barrels per annum, twice the figure imported from Sweden in any year after 1700. Moreover, by 1718 the importation of Swedish pitch and tar to Britain, according to Eleanor Lord, had been reduced to zero. Of the 82,000 barrels, South Carolina provided 52,000, over 60 percent, presumably all dispatched to Britain because of the subsidy. It is amusing, and somewhat ironical, that Eleanor Lord, who provides the total figure, neglected to discover the respective sources. As a result her entire discussion is focused on New England with scarcely more than a line on Carolina, the chief supplier.

One of the puzzling questions is why, between 1705 and 1713, especially in view of the rapid increase after 1713, the British subsidy encouraged such a modest increase in the production of pitch and tar, from 400 barrels to 6,000 barrels. The answer cannot be easily or finally determined. Perhaps land and labor could be more effectively employed in ranch farming and rice; perhaps the internal political quarrels affected individual judgments. More probably, the time

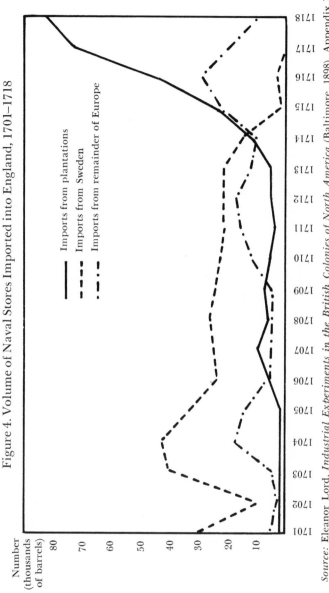

Figure 4. Volume of Naval Stores Imported into England, 1701–1718

Number
(thousands
of barrels)

Imports from plantations
Imports from Sweden
Imports from remainder of Europe

Source: Eleanor Lord, *Industrial Experiments in the British Colonies of North America* (Baltimore, 1898), Appendix B.

limit set when the subsidy was adopted—its original life was to extend nine years, to 1714—inhibited planters from making long-term investments in an enterprise heavily dependent upon British subsidization, but who, when the subsidy was renewed for eleven years beginning 1714, no longer felt restrained.

Whether the prospect of the renewal of the subsidies for naval stores served as the most significant incentive cannot be finally settled, but two new factors enhanced the attractiveness of manufacturing naval stores. The first of these was the conclusion of the War of Spanish Succession, with the Treaty of Utrecht in 1713. The war, which affected every major country in the Western World and its New World colonies, disrupted commerce and communication. The sharp rise in the Carolina export of naval stores in 1714 coincides with the first year of peace. A second factor which reinforced rather than caused the upswing in naval stores was the outbreak of the Yamasee War in 1715, which reduced ranch farming and rice production but left the pine tree with its potential yields of tar and pitch unimpaired and ready for exploitation. Slave-owning planters who needed to find profitable employment for their labor force could and did respond to the most enticing commercial enterprise instantly available, the manufacture of naval stores.[25]

After 1712 slave importation boomed, rising from less than 100 persons annually in 1712 to 600 in 1720, interrupted briefly in 1715 and 1716 by the Yamasee War. The consequence was the final step in the permanent establishment of the plantation system in South Carolina based on slavery.

The statistical correlation between the rise of naval stores and the rapid increase in slaves is corroborated by contemporary observers. Governor Robert Johnson, responding to queries posed by the Board of Trade in 1720, reported:

Figure 5. Number of Slaves Imported into South Carolina, 1706–1724

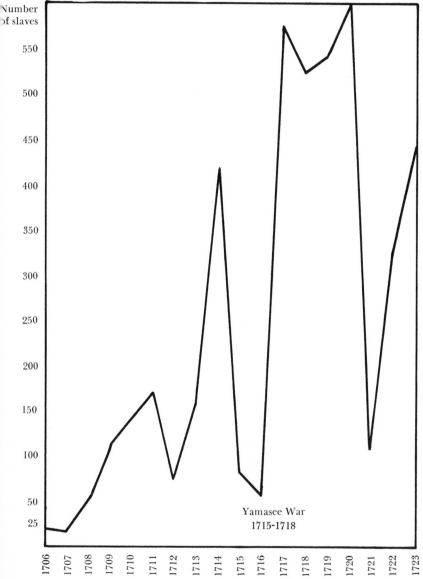

Source: Elizabeth Donnan, *Documents Illustrative of the History of the Slave Trade to America*, 4 vols. (Washington, D.C., 1930).

The . . . Money Granted by Act of Parliament of Great Britain for the importing Pitch, Tarr, Masts and other Navall Stores has been of great encouragement to the Plantations in Generall to export Navall Stores, so this Plantation in particular has Surpassed all America besides in Supplying Great Britain. Accordingly with great quantities of Pitch and Tarr, there have been Exported in one Year by Computation above fifty Thousand Barrells of both which great exports of Navall Stores not only have Occasioned the greater Consumption of British Manufacturers but encouraged the merchants abroad to import into this Province great Numbers of Negro Slaves from Africa and brought a great concourse of ships to this Port to load our bulky commodities. . . . To this bounty Money wee chiefly attribute the Cause of our Trades increasing very Considerably within these Ten Years our Planters having by means thereof been so enriched as to Purchase great Numbers of Negro Slaves the labour of which has incredibly increased the Produce and Manufacture of this Province.[26]

Joseph Boone and John Barnwell, agents for the colony in England, confirmed the Governor's view. "Yet the number of Blacks . . . ," they stated, "have very much increased for the Pitch and Tar Trade prodigiously Increasing have occasioned the Inhabitants to buy Blacks." [27]

The growing prosperity of South Carolina as suggested by these contemporaries can be confirmed by statistical evidence. Taking into consideration free persons, white servants, and slaves, Indian as well as black, the value of exports per capita in 1708 is less than 1 pound 10 shillings. Stated in terms of slaves alone, including slave children, the value of exports is less than 3 pounds 8 shillings per capita. In 1721 exports to Britain per capita were approximately 3 pounds 2 shillings. Stated in terms of slave population alone, exports per capita were 5 pounds 4 shillings. Therefore, the gross value of exports in Carolina per capita doubled between 1708 and 1721. Stated in terms of the number of slaves, it increased 150 percent.[28]

The transformation of the Carolina economy between 1710 and 1720 is starkly revealed in Carolina's contribution to the total value of goods exported to Britain by all the continental colonies. In 1700 Carolina's share was 3 percent. In 1710 it was 5 percent. In 1720 it was 13 percent. The value of South Carolina's imports from Britain, relative to the total imports from Britain to the continental colonies, reveals a different story. In 1700 it was 3 percent. In 1710 it was 5 percent. In 1720 it remained 5 percent.

These figures indicate that capital accumulation was taking place—largely in the form of slaves. Importation of 500 slaves at 20 pounds sterling for each slave, for instance, amounts to 10,000 pounds sterling, approximately the value of the exports in naval stores. The rigidity which this type of investment introduced into the economy was foreseen in an informative pamphlet, *A Letter from South Carolina*, for which Thomas Nairne reputedly prepared the materials. It

Figure 6. South Carolina's Share of Total Value of Exports to and Imports from Great Britain

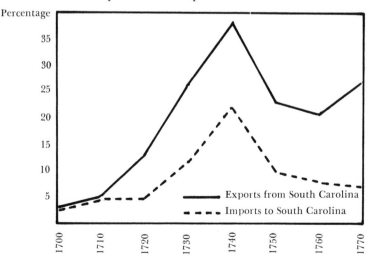

indicated the expenditures a planter could anticipate in order to get started in South Carolina on a major scale:

Figure 7. Investment Required to Settle an Estate
of 300 Pounds Per Annum

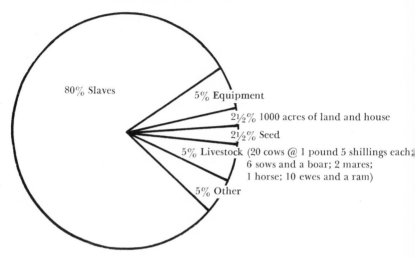

80% Slaves

5% Equipment

2½% 1000 acres of land and house

2½% Seed

5% Livestock (20 cows @ 1 pound 5 shillings each;
6 sows and a boar; 2 mares;
1 horse; 10 ewes and a ram)

5% Other

Total: 1500 pounds (South Carolina money)
1000 pounds (sterling)

Source: [Thomas Nairne], *A Letter from South Carolina* (1710)

VI

On the basis of the evidence provided in this essay, the following conclusions are warranted:

One, the issue of white attitudes toward blacks in early South Carolina is an open rather than a closed question, with the period 1715–1720 serving as the transition years.

Two, blacks were regarded as highly capable in war and peace.

Three, slavery and the plantation system were confined to the Carolina low country during the colonial period.

Four, the production of naval stores played the decisive role in the development of the plantation system in South Carolina.

Five, slave importation as the base of the plantation system correlates with the rise of naval stores.

Six, all elements associated with the plantation system—the plantation family as a social institution, the role of white and black women within the family and society, and the place of the family in the political-economic-social life of the colony, to list obvious examples—were affected by the development of naval stores as a commercial product for which slave labor was imported.

Seven, increased slave importation introduced an inflexibility into the South Carolina economy—in terms of capital assets as well as productive capacity—which historians recognize but tend to understate.

Eight, the gross importation of slaves triggered by the rising production of naval stores increased the fear of black power—"to the great endangering to the Province" wrote the agents of South Carolina—and led to the political response of the 1720s to propose and execute a township system to contain the territorial limits of slavery, thereby attempting to moderate its social-economic effect.

Nine, South Carolina's prosperity made it an increasingly opportune target for a takeover by the royal government and each of its major exports—deerskins, rice, and naval stores—fitted neatly into official British mercantile policies.

What does this external evidence fail to reveal? It does not tell us about the makeup or development of a single plantation or a group of plantations. It does not reveal the fabric of the family. It does not indicate the role of parish or colony politics. It provides no insight into the function of the church. It does not even suggest the distribution among whites of the increase in productivity and income. Yet the external evidence tells us much more about the internal society than we would otherwise know, and it reinforces the thrust of these essays that, underlying all the variances of the colonial South, is a central theme, the southern mosaic.

Notes

ONE—*The Political Background of Proprietary Carolina*

1. John Stewart to Major William Dunlop, 27 April 1690, in "Letters from John Stewart to William Dunlop," in *The South Carolina Historical and Genealogical Magazine* (Baltimore), XXXII, no. 1 (January 1931), 15.

2. For convenience the terms South Carolina and North Carolina are used to distinguish the two regions that eventually became separate and distinct colonies, although the proprietors regarded the Carolinas as an entity.

3. William James Rivers, *A Sketch of the History of South Carolina to the Close of the Proprietary Government by the Revolution of 1719* (Charleston, 1856), chapter 6. Rivers was the first scholar to appreciate the dimensions of South Carolina politics, and on many points he is more dependable in his judgments than later and more impassioned scholars. Invaluable contemporary documents are reprinted in the Appendix of Rivers's volume. Four other scholars should be mentioned at the outset: Edward McCrady, *The History of South Carolina under the Proprietary Government, 1670–1719* (New York, 1897); David Duncan Wallace, *The History of South Carolina*, 4 vols. (New York, 1934), I; M. Eugene Sirmans, *Colonial South Carolina: A Political History, 1663–1763* (Chapel Hill, 1966); and Converse D. Clowse, *Economic Beginnings in Colonial South Carolina, 1670–1730* (Columbia, 1971).

4. John Stewart to Major William Dunlop, 27 April 1690, in "Letters from John Stewart," pp. 9, 12, 13.

5. Ibid., pp. 9, 10.

6. Ibid., pp. 13, 27.

7. Nathaniel Johnson was to influence politics in South Carolina. See *Dictionary of National Biography*, X, 111. For quotation: "Letters from John Stewart," pp. 14–15.

8. Ibid., p. 29.

9. Ibid., p. 11. One hundred men signed the petition to invoke martial law.

10. Wallace, *The History of South Carolina*, I, 117–118.

11. Rivers, *A Sketch of the History of South Carolina*, p. 428.

12. Ibid., p. 424.

13. Ibid., pp. 425–426.

14. *Ibid.*, p. 424.

15. Sothell was notified of his suspension as governor of North Carolina in

Lords Proprietors to Sothell, 2 December 1689 (London), in *North Carolina Colonial Records*, I, 359–360. The list of grievances against Sothell is enclosed in a letter from Lords Proprietors to Sothell, 12 May 1691 (London), in Ibid., I, 367–371.

16. Thomas Cooper, ed., *The Statutes at Large of South Carolina* (Columbia, 1837), II, 39–73. The Carolina Parliament was composed of the Grand Council, made up of caciques and landgraves who were deputies of proprietors and of delegates elected by freemen. Before Sothell, as an earlier petition from Carolina makes clear, seven delegates, members of the Commons House, were out-voted by eight members of the council on any controversial issue.

17. Proprietors to James Colleton, 13 May 1691, in Alexander Salley, ed., *Commissions and Instructions from the Lords Proprietors of Carolina* (printed for Historical Commission of South Carolina, Columbia, 1916), pp. 27–28. Proprietors to Governor, Deputies, and Grand Council, 27 May 1691, in ibid., pp. 17–18; Cooper, *Statutes*, II, 44–47.

18. Nullification of Acts of "Assembly or pretended parliament" in Proprietors to Governor "for the time being" of South Carolina, 22 September 1691, in *Records in British Public Record Office* (Atlanta, 1931), III, 31–32. For "outing . . . of their Rights," Proprietors to Seth Sothell, 12 May 1691, recorded 28 May 1692, in Salley, *Commissions and Instructions from Lord Proprietors of Carolina*, p. 30.

19. Appointment of Ludwell, Proprietors to Ludwell, 2 November 1691, ibid., p. 33.

20. The best modern edition of the six versions of the Fundamental Constitutions is printed in *North Carolina Charters and Constitutions, 1578–1698* (edited by Mattie Erma Edwards Parker), Carolina Charter Tercentenary Commission, Raleigh, 1963, pp. 128–240.

21. Ibid., pp. 74–104. The specific quotation is from p. 95. A similar clause appears in the Charter of 1663.

22. Mattie Erma Edwards Parker in the introductory essay to the various versions of the Fundamental Constitutions suggests rather than declares that Locke played a secondary rather than primary role. Parker, *North Carolina Charters*, pp. 128–131. Confer with conclusions of others, some of them differing from judgment made in the text. Maurice Cranston, *John Locke: A Biography* (London, 1957), pp. 119ff; Louis Fargo Brown, *The First Earl of Shaftesbury* (New York, 1933), pp. 156–161; Herbert R. Paschal, "Proprietary North Carolina: A Study in Colonial Government" (diss., University of North Carolina, 1961), pp. 117–118; M. Eugene Sirmans, "Masters of Ashley Hall: A Biographical study of the Bull Family of South Carolina, 1670–1737" (diss., Princeton University, 1959), pp. 12–23.

23. Parker, ed., *North Carolina Charters*, p. 94.

24. Rivers, *A Sketch of the History of South Carolina*, pp. 422–423.

25. John Stewart to William Dunlop in "Letters from John Stewart," pp. 9–10.

26. Parker, ed., *North Carolina Charters*, p. 181.

27. Paschal, "Proprietary North Carolina: A Study in Colonial Government," pp. 129, 133, 281ff.

28. *The Journal of the Commons House of Assembly of South Carolina,* passim.

29. Petition to Seth Sothell, Rivers, *Proprietary South Carolina,* p. 422.

30. A. S. Salley, indexer, *Records in the British Public Record Office Relating to South Carolina, 1691–1697* (Atlanta, 1931), III, 105–106.

31. The original instructions called for twenty members of the assembly to be divided equally between Berkeley, Colleton, Craven (South Carolina), and Albemarle (North Carolina) counties. But this instruction was superseded by the 7–7–6 ratio. Salley, Jr., ed., *Journal of the Commons House of Assembly of South Carolina for the Session Beginning September 20, 1692, and Ending October 15, 1692* (Columbia, 1907), 12 October 1692, pp. 22–23. The Commons House had returned delegates according to the 7–7–6 ratio at the beginning of the session in late September. Proprietors to Governor Ludwell, 12 April 1693, in Salley, indexer, *Records in the British Public Record Office,* III, 84–98. First quotation pp. 92–93, second quotation p. 93.

32. It is noteworthy that when the Commons House of Assembly confronted the issue of the Fundamental Constitutions, the delegation sent to speak with Governor Ludwell was balanced between Berkeley and Colleton county men. *Journals of the Commons House, September 20, 1692–October 15, 1692,* passim.

33. Sirmans, "Masters of Ashley Hall: A Biographical Study of the Bull Family of Colonial South Carolina, 1670–1737," p. 64.

34. Salley, ed., *Journals of the Commons House of Assembly of South Carolina for the Four Sessions of 1693.* (Columbia, 1907), 18 January 1693, p. 17.

35. John Archdale, *Narrative; A New Description of that Fertile and Pleasant Province of Carolina: With a Brief Account of its Discovery and Settling, and the Government Thereof to this Time,* "With several Remarkable Passages of *Divine Providence* during my time." Printed in 1707, reprinted in B. R. Carroll, ed., *Historical Collections of South Carolina; embracing many rare and valuable pamphlets, and other documents, relating to the history of that state from its first discovery to its independence, in the year 1776,* 2 vols. (New York, 1836), II, 85–120. For the background of the discussion among the proprietors, see p. 102.

36. William Stevens Powell, *The Proprietors of Carolina* (Raleigh, 1963), pp. 51–52.

37. John Archdale, *Narrative; A New Description,* reprinted in Carroll, ed., *Historical Collections of South Carolina,* II, 103.

38. Instructions to John Archdale, 31 August 1694, in Salley, indexer, *Records in the British Public Record Office Relating to South Carolina, 1691–1697* (Atlanta, 1931), III, 140–142; Cooper, ed., *The Statutes at Large of South Carolina,* II, 96–104. Cooper is in error in dating of An Act to Ascertain Prices, p. 102. See Salley, ed., *Journal of the Commons House of Assembly of South Carolina for the Session Beginning January 30, 1696, and Ending March 17, 1696* (Columbia, 1908), 16 March 1696, pp. 45–46.

39. Proprietors to Philip Ludwell, 12 April 1693, in Salley, indexer, *Records in the British Public Record Office,* III, 88.

40. Cooper, ed., *The Statutes at Large of South Carolina,* II, 102–104.

41. Salley, ed., *Journal of the Commons House of Assembly of South Carolina, For the Session Beginning January 30, 1696, and Ending March 17, 1696* (Columbia, 1908), 17 March 1696.

42. Proprietors to John Archdale, 29 January 1696, in Salley, indexer, *Records in the British Public Record Office*, III, 167.

43. Cooper, ed., *The Statutes at Large of South Carolina*, II, 101–102.

44. Paschal, "Proprietary North Carolina: A Study in Colonial Government," pp. 99–109.

45. Proprietors to Messers Trouillard, Buretell, Jacques Serrurier, Couraw, Vervant, De Lisle Cramahe, Duque, 12 April 1693, in Salley, indexer, *Records in the British Public Record Office Relating to South Carolina, 1691–1697*, III, 103–104; Proclamation of Proprietors, 12 April 1693, in ibid., III, 82. The timing of the act may be related to the Treaty of Ryswick between France and England which was concluded the same year. The terms did not confront the question of the political rights of the Huguenots, no doubt a deliberate omission. As a result this issue became entangled in the struggle for political power among Carolinians.

46. Cooper, ed., *The Statutes at Large of South Carolina*, II, 131–133.

47. Salley, ed., *Journals of the Commons House of Assembly of South Carolina for the Two Sessions of 1698* (Columbia, 1914), 19 November 1698.

TWO—*Internal Politics in Proprietary Carolina*

1. Arthur Henry Hirsch, *The Huguenots of Colonial South Carolina* (Durham, 1928), passim.

2. In any analysis of the inner struggle for political power within South Carolina the term "Goose Creek Men" inevitably arises. It has been used sparingly in this essay because it tends to mislead. The designation has become a catchall, indeed, almost a code word, so loosely defined as to hinder rather than help an understanding of events.

Not well informed as to the true situation of Carolina politics in the 1690s —and even less so after 1700—the proprietors often mistakenly designated the "Goose Creek Men" as the sole source of antiproprietory feeling. Unfortunately, historians, from the first to the most recent, have been inclined to reinforce this misperception by using the term "Goose Creek Men" or "Goose Creek coalition" as if this group were, in fact, the key to explain what was happening—an assumption far off the mark. As the previous essay demonstrates, a discriminating analysis of the politics of the 1690s reveals that opposition to proprietary rule was so widespread as to encompass almost all colonials and that they stood unified on the principle of self-government. The term "Goose Creek Men" is seldom employed in the present essay, not because of any arbitrary personal decision but rather because a thorough examination of the contemporary evidence does not provide a solid foundation to sustain its use.

3. The analysis in this essay differs in concept and many details from authorities such as David Duncan Wallace, *The History of South Carolina*, 4 vols. (New York, 1934), I, passim; Edward McCrady, *The History of*

South Carolina under the Proprietary Government, 1670–1719 (New York, 1897), passim; and M. Eugene Sirmans, *Colonial South Carolina; A Political History, 1663–1763* (Chapel Hill, 1966).

4. This analysis is based principally on a close study of the *Journal of the Commons House of Assembly of South Carolina*, particularly the composition of its membership over two decades as well as the limited extant correspondence of political leaders which illuminates the question of political allegiance.

5. Archdale and Council to Proprietors, 2 October 1695, in A. S. Salley, Jr., ed., *Commissions and Instructions from the Lords Proprietors of Carolina to Public Officials of South Carolina, 1685–1715* (Columbia, 1916), 85; A. S. Salley, Jr., ed., *Journal of the Commons House of Assembly of South Carolina for the Session Beginning January 30, 1696, and Ending March 17, 1696* (Columbia, 1908), 30 January 1696. The writ was issued 30 November 1695, with an election date set for 19 December 1695, in Charleston, but a second writ was issued dated 20 December 1695.

6. Governor Archdale and Council to Proprietors, 20 August 1695, in Salley, ed., *Commissions and Instructions*, pp. 80–81.

7. Governor Archdale and Council to Proprietors, 28 August 1696, in Salley, ed., *Commissions and Instructions*, p. 94.

8. Hirsch, *The Huguenots of Colonial South Carolina*, pp. 111-120. Whereas the English-Anglicans had nothing to fear from the Crown, Dissenters were unduly responsive to royal regulations to avoid an imputation on their management of the King's interest and the proprietary interest.

9. William James Rivers, *A Sketch of the History of South Carolina to the Close of the Proprietary Government by the Revolution of 1719* (Charleston, 1856), p. 194.

10. A. S. Salley, Jr., ed., *Journal of the Commons House of Assembly of South Carolina For the Session Beginning October 30, 1700 and Ending November 16, 1700* (Columbia, 1924), 30 October 1700; "The Representation and Address of several of the Members of this present Assembly return'd for Colleton County, and the other Inhabitants of this Province . . . ," to the Proprietors, printed in Rivers, *A Sketch of the History of South Carolina*, pp. 453–460. The quotation is from p. 455.

11. Salley, ed., *Journal of the Commons House of Assembly of South Carolina for the Session Beginning October 30, 1700 and Ending November 16, 1700* (Columbia, 1924), 30 October 1700; Salley, ed., *Journals of the Commons House of Assembly of South Carolina for the Two Sessions of 1698* (Columbia, 1914), 13 September 1698. A pamphlet written by Thomas Nairne, a gifted leader in Colleton County, claimed that two thirds of the population of South Carolina was composed of Dissenters. He included the French Huguenots in this definition. If his estimate is correct, it is not confirmed by recorded votes either before or after 1700.

12. Salley, ed., *Journal of the Commons House of Assembly of South Carolina For the Session Beginning October 30, 1700 and Ending November 16, 1700* (Columbia, 1924), 30 October 1700 and 16 November 1700, passim.

13. "The Representation and Address of several of the Members of this

138 *Notes*

present Assembly return'd for Colleton County, and other the Inhabitants
of this Province," printed in Rivers, *A Sketch of the History of South
Carolina,* p. 459. See also John Ash, *The Present State of Affairs in Carolina,
1706* in Alexander S. Salley, Jr., ed., *Narratives of Early Carolina, 1650–1708*
(New York, 1911), p. 271.

14. Salley, ed., *Journal of the Commons House of Assembly of South
Carolina for the Session Beginning August 13, 1701 and Ending August 28,
1701* (Columbia, 1926), 19 August 1701; Salley, ed., *Journals of the Commons House of Assembly of South Carolina for 1702* (Columbia, 1932), 4
April 1702; ibid., 26 August 1702.

15. "The Representation and Address of several of the Members of this
present Assembly return'd for Colleton County, and other the Inhabitants
of this Province . . . ," printed in Rivers, *A Sketch of the History of South
Carolina,* p. 454.

16. Ibid., pp. 459, 455, 460.

17. Ibid., pp. 455–458; Salley, ed., *Journals of the Commons House of
Assembly of South Carolina for the Two Sessions of 1698* (Columbia, 1914),
13 September 1698. The Representation as printed in Rivers spells the name
as George Dearsby, whereas the *Journals* spells it as Dearsley.

18. John Archdale, *A New Description of That Fertile and Pleasant Province of Carolina: With a Brief Account of its Discovery and Setting, and the
Government Thereof to This Time; with Several Remarkable Passage of
Divine Providence during My Time* in B. R. Carroll, ed., *Historical Collections of South Carolina,* II, 112.

19. Thomas Cooper, ed., *The Statutes at Large of South Carolina* (Columbia, 1837), II, 232.

20. Ibid., pp. 236–246.

21. Ibid., pp. 249–251.

22. The contemporary account used most widely by historians, usually
without noting that it was the source of their information and conclusion,
is that of Daniel Defoe, *Party-Tyranny, or an Occasional Bill in Miniature;
as now Practiced in Carolina; Humbly offered to the Consideration of both
Houses of Parliament* (London, 1705), printed in Alexander S. Salley, Jr.
ed., *Narratives of Early Carolina, 1650–1708* (New York, 1911), pp. 224–264.
Defoe depended on the information given him which was, of course, provided largely by the Dissenter petitioners. The partisanship is easy to dis-
count, but the grave inaccuracies, many difficult to establish, have misled
later historians. For example, every historian writing of these events as-
sumes, on the basis of Defoe and the petitioners' account in the House of
Lords, that the proprietors validated the act. Perhaps so. But a document,
entirely overlooked by historians, provides persuasive contrary evidence.
It is a letter from the Lords Proprietors to Governor Johnson, dated 6
March 1705. Its substance is as follows:

Whereas an Act was past in Carolina and Signed and Sealed by Sir
Nathaniell Johnson as Governor Thomas Broughton, James Moore,
Nicholas Trott, Robt. Gibbs and Henry Noble our Deputies En-
tituled as following

South Carolina

An Act for the Establishment of Religious Worship in this Province according to the Church of England and for the Erecting of Churches for the Worship of God and also for the Maintenance of Ministers and the Building convenient houses for them
Which said Act Wee the Palatine and Lords Proprietors Do discent to and hereby make Null and Void and Require you not to put the same in Execution as a Law. Given under our hands and Seales this Sixth day of March 1705.

> Granville Palatine
> M. Ashley
> J. Colleton
> Jo. Archdale

[A. S. Salley, indexer, *Records in the British Public Record Office Relating to South Carolina, 1701–1710* (Columbia, 1947), V, 140–141.]

There can be no question but that this document refers to the Church Act because the list of its signatures is accurate. The document is dated before the appeal in Parliament and certainly preceded any order from the Crown.

The contemporary accounts are so notoriously inaccurate that collaborative evidence is needed, point by point. It is even possible to raise a question as to whether John Ash preceded Boone and died in England, as stated by contemporaries. John Ash's name appears repeatedly in the *Journals of the Commons House* after 1706. Presumably, this is the son or relative of John Ash of Dissenter fame, but no historian has explained the repeated appearance of the name.

The proprietors may have been moved to invalidate the Church Act because of the power of the Ecclesiastical Commissioners.

No evidence indicates that the Exclusion Act was nullified by the proprietors, so that the appeal made to Parliament for its moderation or invalidation corresponds with other evidence to suggest that the Exclusion Act was the key to the intracolonial struggle for power.

23. Petition of Joseph Boone et al., 28 February 1706, in Leo F. Stock, ed., *Proceedings and Debates of the British Parliament Respecting North America, 1542–1754, 5 vols.* (Washington, 1924–1941), III, 117. The petitioners made much of having only twenty-three members of the Commons House present, but to have six or seven members absent was common rather than unusual; quote from Rivers, *A Sketch of the History of South Carolina*, p. 462.

24. Daniel Defoe, *Party-Tyranny* printed in Salley, ed., *Narratives of Early Carolina, 1650–1708* (New York, 1911), pp. 225–226.

25. Sirmans, *Colonial South Carolina*, p. 88.

26. Salley, *Journal of the Commons House of Assembly of South Carolina, March 6, 1705/6–April 9, 1706* (Columbia, 1937), 7 March 1706.

27. Cooper, ed., *The Statutes at Large of South Carolina*, II, "An Act for the Establishment of Religious Worship in the Province, According to the Church of England, and for the Erecting of Churches for the Publick Worship of God, and Also for the Maintenance of Ministers and the Building Convenient Houses for them" (1706), pp. 282–294, and "An Additional Act

to an Act Entituled An Act for the Establishment of Religious Worship in this Province According to the Church of England, and for the Erecting of Churches for the Public Worship of God, and Also for the Maintenance of Ministers and the Building Convenient Houses for Them" (1708), pp. 328–330.

28. Salley, *Journals of the Commons House of Assembly of South Carolina for 1703* (Columbia, 1934), 13 January–24 February 1703, passim; ibid., 15 April 1703.

29. Verner W. Crane, *The Southern Frontier, 1670–1732* (Durham, 1928), pp. 71–107.

30. Salley, ed., *Journals of the Commons House of Assembly of South Carolina for the Two Sessions of 1698* (Columbia, 1914), 18 November 1698.

31. Salley, ed., *Journal of the Commons House of Assembly of South Carolina, November 20, 1706–February 8, 1706/7* (Columbia, 1939), 31 January 1707.

32. Salley, ed., *Journal of the Commons House of Assembly of South Carolina, June 5, 1707–July 19, 1707* (Columbia, 1940), 5 July 1707.

33. Cooper, ed., *The Statutes at Large of South Carolina*, II, 309–316; Salley, ed., *Journal of the Commons House of Assembly of South Carolina, June 5, 1707–July 19, 1707* (Columbia, 1940), 19 July 1707.

34. Crane, *Southern Frontier*, pp. 146–150. The position taken by the governor had nothing whatsoever to do with a contest between the proprietary authority and the Commons House, as is often asserted. Appearances represented reality: Governor Johnson's private greed prompted him to take the position that he did. On this issue, he did not receive support from the English-Anglican political bloc.

35. Two general accounts are valuable. Stephen B. Weeks, *The Religious Development in the Province of North Carolina* in *Johns Hopkins University Studies*, Tenth Series, V–VI (1892), 241–306; Herbert R. Paschal, Jr., "Proprietary North Carolina; A Study in Colonial Government" (Diss., University of North Carolina, 1961).

36. Lieutenant Governor Alexander Spotswood to Lords of Trade, 11 February 1713, in William L. Saunders, ed., *The Colonial Records of North Carolina* (Raleigh, 1886), II, 1713 to 1728, 12.

37. Declaration of Captain John Gibbs, 2 June 1690, in Saunders, ed., *Colonial Records of North Carolina*, I, 363–364.

38. Paschal, "Proprietary North Carolina," 179–180.

39. Henderson Walker to the Bishop of London, 21 October 1703 in Saunders, ed., *The Colonial Records of North Carolina*, I, 572; see also, 543–545. The act is not extant. Its provisions as reconstructed from other evidence are provided in Weeks, *The Religious Development in the Province of North Carolina*, p. 36.

40. John Blair to the Society for the Propagation of the Gospel in Foreign Parts (1703), in Saunders, ed., *The Colonial Records of North Carolina*, I, 601–602.

41. Henderson Walker to the Bishop of London, 21 October 1703, in Saunders ed., *The Colonial Records of North Carolina*, I, 572; John Blair to the Society for the Propagation of the Gospel in Foreign Parts, ibid., p. 601.

42. Weeks, *The Religious Development in the Province of North Carolina*, pp. 48–49.

43. The Reverend William Gordon to the Society for the Propagation of the Gospel in Foreign Parts, 13 May 1709, in Saunders, ed., *The Colonial Records of North Carolina*, I, 709.

44. The Reverend John Urmston[e] to the Society for the Propagation of the Gospel in Foreign Parts, 7 July 1711, in ibid., I, 769.

45. An Act for the better and more effectual preserving the Queen's peace . . . , 1711, in ibid., I, 787–790; Alexander Spotswood to the Board of Trade, 25 July 1711, in ibid., I, 780.

46. Alexander Spotswood to the Lords Proprietors, 31 July 1711, in ibid., I, 800.

47. The most thorough and accurate survey of the county courts in North Carolina is Paul M. McCain, *The County Court in North Carolina Before 1750* (Durham, 1954), in *Historical Papers of Trinity College Historical Society*, Series XXXI. North Carolina county and precinct courts receive some attention in John Spencer Bassett, *The Constitutional Beginnings of North Carolina, 1663–1729*, in *Johns Hopkins University Studies in Historical and Political Science* (Baltimore, 1894), Twelfth Series, pp. 105–169. References to precinct courts are found on pp. 105–106, 124, and 165. It is not surprising that no comparable volume to McCain's on local government is to be found for South Carolina. Two other books merit mention: William C. Guess, *County Government in Colonial North Carolina*, in *James Sprunt Studies*, XI, no. 1 (1911), 7–39, and especially David L. Corbitt, *The Formation of North Carolina Counties, 1663–1943* (Raleigh, 1950).

48. McCain, *The County Courts in North Carolina Before 1750*, p. 11.

49. Ibid., passim.

50. *Calendar of State Papers, Colonial Series 31, America and the West Indies, January 1719 to February 1720*, pp. 337–338.

51. Sirmans, *Colonial South Carolina*, pp. 142–143. In the debates on the act there was a difference of opinion as to the limits of the jurisdiction of the county-precinct courts. See, for example: *Journal of the Upper House*, I, 78, and An Act for Establishing County and Precinct Courts in David J. McCord, ed., *The Statutes at Large of South Carolina*, VII, 166–176.

52. The quote is found in McCain, *The County Court in North Carolina Before 1750*, p. 11. McCain recognizes the influence of the Fundamental Constitutions on North Carolina; but because he makes no comparisons with what transpires in South Carolina, the differences are not noted.

THREE—*Reassessing the Founding of Georgia*

1. John C. Stephens, Jr., ed., *Georgia, and Two Other Occasional Poems on the Founding of the Colony, 1736* (Atlanta, 1950), 9–10. See also the verse written in the *South Carolina Gazette*, upon the settling of Georgia. Hennig Cohen, "Two Colonial Poems on the Settling of Georgia," in *Georgia Historical Quarterly*, XXXVII (1953), 129–137.

The conclusions developed in this essay are based principally on an exhaustive investigation of the published and unpublished primary sources. In the latter category special mention should be made of the Egmont Papers in the University of Georgia Library. The library staff and Professor E. M. Coulter made this rich treasure available to me before it was opened to scholars, and I am greatly indebted to them for their kindness and generosity. In the interval between the opening of the papers and now, some of this source material has been published by the University of Georgia Press supported by the Wormsloe Foundation. Scholars will continue to be beholden to the press and the foundation for recognizing the significance of these materials. For the trusteeship period Georgia has probably the most complete record available for any colony in British North America during its "founding" decades, because the frequent, indeed, often daily, responses kept by the inhabitants and by the trustees have been preserved.

Space precludes doing full justice to scholars of colonial Georgia who precede me, but the citations in this essay indicate a small measure of my obligation to them. Their work has unquestionably influenced in some degree the conclusions drawn in this essay.

2. Thomas Causton to his wife, 12 March 1733, in Egmont Papers (University of Georgia), Vol. 14200.

3. The best modern study is Amos E. Ettinger, *James Edward Oglethorpe: Imperial Idealist* (Oxford, 1936). It must now be supplemented, however, by materials that have since become available.

4. *The Diary of the Earl of Egmont* serves as a running account of the founding of Georgia, which his papers, now at the University of Georgia, amplify. Historical Manuscripts Commission, *Manuscripts of the Earl of Egmont. Diary of Viscount Percival, afterwards First Earl of Egmont*, 3 vols. (London, 1920–1923); for Charter, Allen D. Chandler, comp., *The Colonial Records of the State of Georgia* (Atlanta, 1904), I, 11–26.

5. The two points of view are admirably stated in Verner W. Crane, "The Philanthropists and the Genesis of Georgia," *American Historical Review*, XXVII (1921–1922), 63–69, and in Albert B. Saye, *New Viewpoints in Georgia History* (Athens, 1943), 3–50.

6. It would be difficult to explain why Oglethorpe laid out settlements in such remote scattered areas, except as a fulfillment of his concept of defense. When he laid out the settlement at Thunderbolt, for example, he stated that this tactic "guarded the most dangerous Water Passage from the Spaniards." Oglethorpe to Trustees, c. December 1733 in Egmont Papers, Vol. 14200. At times Oglethorpe's aggressive tactics provoked light reprimands from the trustees. For instance, the trustees, in 1736, asked Oglethorpe to withdraw the Highlanders from the Alatamaha River region and settle them nearer Savannah. Benjamin Martyn to James Oglethorpe, 2 April 1736, ibid., Vol. 14208.

7. Paul S. Taylor, *Georgia Plan: 1732–1752* (Berkeley, 1972), p. 3.

8. Allen D. Candler, comp., *The Colonial Records of the State of Georgia* (Atlanta, 1904–1916), I, 48.

9. Ibid., III, 373, 374.

10. Ibid., I, 50.

11. Earl of Egmont to General Oglethorpe, 11 March 1742, Egmont Papers, Vol. 14206.

12. George Fenwick Jones, ed., *Detailed Reports on the Salzburger Emigrants Who Settled in America . . . Edited by Samuel Urlsperger* (Athens, 1968), I, 57ff.

13. The names of the first group can be found in E. Merton Coulter, ed., "A List of the First Shipload of Georgia Settlers," in *Georgia Historical Quarterly*, XXXI (1947), 282–288.

14. Governor Robert Johnson, Charlestown, to Oglethorpe, 28 September 1732, Egmont Papers, Vol. 14200.

15. Benjamin Martyn to Governor Johnson, 24 January 1733, ibid., Vol. 14207. The specific agreements and instructions for the voyage can be found in this volume of manuscripts.

16. Martyn to Johnson, 18 October 1732, ibid., Vol. 14207; Johnson to Oglethorpe, 28 September 1732, ibid., Vol. 14200.

17. Thomas Causton to his wife, 12 March 1733, ibid., Vol. 14200.

18. Oglethorpe to Trustees, 12 March 1733, ibid., Vol. 14200.

19. Oglethorpe to Trustees, 12 August 1733, ibid., Vol. 14200.

20. See Adelaide L. Fries, *The Moravians in Georgia, 1735–1740* (Raleigh, 1905).

21. Governor Johnson to Trustees, 27 July 1733, Egmont Papers, Vol. 14200.

22. For the oldest yet useful study on the Salzburgers, see Philip A. Strobel, *The Salzburgers and Their Descendents: Being the history of a colony of German (Lutheran) Protestants, who Emigrated to Georgia in 1734, and settled at Ebenezer, twenty-five miles above the City of Savannah* (Baltimore, 1855). See also Paul Taylor, Klaus G. Leowald, and Beverly Starika, eds., "Johann Martin Bolzius Answers a Questionnaire on Carolina and Georgia" in *William and Mary Quarterly*, XIV (April 1957), 218–261. In recent years an increasing number of sources relating to the experience of the Salzburgers is being published. Reverend Bolzius to Mr. Newman, secretary to the Society for Christian Knowledge, 29 December 1740, Egmont Papers, Vol. 14205. The precise number was 189 people, men, women, and children. The number of Salzburgers has often been grossly inflated by historians of colonial Georgia. Oglethorpe reflected the general opinion when he wrote that every foreign person settled in America was worth thirty pounds sterling per annum in terms of trade and production. Oglethorpe to Egmont, 1 February 1736, Egmont Papers, Vol. 14201.

23. John Vat to Mr. Newman, 10 February 1735, Egmont Papers, Vol. 14200.

24. Reverend Bolzius to Captain Coram, 28 July 1737, ibid., Vol. 14203. A record is also available of the Salzburgers' "Account With the Trustees," which, from March 1736 to April 1738 totaled 1,287.17.10½ pounds of which 1,076.10½ pounds was for food. Ibid., Vol. 14203.

25. Oglethorpe to Vernon, 26 January 1741, ibid., Vol. 14205.

26. There are numerous articles on the experimental trustees' garden, but perhaps the best is James W. Holland, "The Beginning of Public Agricultural Experimentation in America: The Trustees Garden in Georgia" in *Agricultural History*, XII (1938), 271–298. This article can be supplemented by other materials. See Trustees Agreement with Dr. Patrick Houstoun, Botanist, 4 October 1732, Egmont Papers, Vol. 14207. In addition, see In-

structions to Dr. Millar, Botanist, 6 March 1734, Egmont Papers, Vol. 14207.

27. The trustees' store was usually well stocked with goods, tools, implements, cooking utensils, provisions, and livestock. See, for example, Inventory of Goods at Trustee's Store, 29 September 1738, Egmont Papers, Vol. 14203.

28. Thomas Christie to Oglethorpe, 14 December 1734, ibid., Vol. 14200.

29. James R. McCain, *Georgia as a Proprietary Province* (Boston, 1917), pp. 29–56.

30. To "give more weight and Distinction to the court," the magistrates were sent a seal and proper gowns. Verelst to Causton, 11 August 1737, Egmont Papers, Vol. 14209. A town court for Frederica was appointed in September 1735, but it did not function satisfactorily. Savannah continued to be the only operating center of government. The Salzburgers, because of their peculiar social-religious community, policed themselves; it is interesting to notice, however, that the Reverend Bolzius eventually asked for the necessary authority to conduct its local government, for he was apprehensive that his religious authority was no longer sufficient or effective.

31. Robert Parker to Trustees, (?) December 1734, ibid., Vol. 14200.

32. Eveleigh to Oglethorpe, 16 May 1735, ibid.

33. Bolzius to Vernon, 13 July 1734, ibid. When the Salzburgers did complain about hardships, Benjamin Martyn, the secretary to the trustees, replied in sardonic, nasty tone: "They [the Salzburgers] are sorry likewise that many of them (as you say) left their good States they lived in by the care of their good Benefactors in Germany, and if the Trustees had known the Goodness of their States they would not by any means have taken them from them." Martyn to Bolzius, 10 June 1736, ibid., Vol. 14208.

34. James Habersham to George Whitefield, 1 September 1741, ibid., Vol. 14206.

35. Thomas Eyre to Robert Eyre, 4 December 1740, ibid., Vol. 14205.

36. William Stephens served the trustees the longest and the most faithfully. For the most appreciative summary of Stephens's service, see the Introduction to E. Merton Coulter, ed., *The Journal of William Stephens, 1741–1743* (Athens, 1958). Journal of Thomas Causton, 31 May 1737, Egmont Papers, Vol. 14203. Thomas Jones to Jo. Lydes, 18 September 1740, ibid., Vol. 14205.

37. Of those who signed the memorial, approximately one half were sent by the trustees, and about one half had arrived in Georgia on their own account. An estimated two thirds of those signing the petition came from the Savannah region, which could be expected for Savannah had the largest population. The signers varied in profession from gentlemen to perukemakers and stocking-makers. Of the signers, however, only fifteen signed with "a mark," indicating that they were unable to write their names. For materials used in this analysis, see ibid., Vol. 14203. Tailfer and a few others had made a request to permit Negroes in Georgia as early as 1735. Tailfer et al. to Trustees, 27 August 1735, ibid., Vol. 14201.

38. The estimate of five hundred is based on the coefficient customarily used to multiply the number of tithables, men between sixteen and sixty, by three or, in some instances, four. Because the signers were all mature men,

the coefficient of four would produce a more accurate estimate of the total population they represented.

39. Trustees' Answer to Representation of 9 December 1738, Egmont Papers, Vol. 14210. This idea of a properly instituted constitution had been expressed as early as 1735 in reply to a letter of Samuel Eveleigh, the Carolina merchant, who had suggested Negro slaves be used. "Sir," the secretary to the Trust had written, "The very end for which the Trustees were incorporated was to procure that Blessing of a well constituted Government, which is so little known in some Parts of America." Martyn to Eveleigh, 1 May 1735, Egmont Papers, Vol. 14207. Oglethorpe had encouraged the cavalier treatment of the memorial by saying everyone had signed because Robert Williams, a merchant, had promised each signer that he would sell them slaves in return for a mortgage on the land of the signers. Oglethorpe to Trustees, 16 January 1739, ibid., Vol. 14203. It should be noted that many signers did not have sufficient land to encourage such alienation, and, with many others, the soil in the grants that they had received would not inspire the confidence of a merchant to extend credit.

40. Oglethorpe, State of Georgia, 11 October 1739, ibid., Vol. 14204; "A State of the Province of Georgia Attested Under Oath in the Court of Savannah November 10, 1740," in *Collections of the Georgia Historical Society* (1842), II, 67–85. It appeared originally in pamphlet form in 1742.

41. Remonstrance of the Inhabitants of the Town and County of Savannah and the Rest of the Inhabitants of Georgia, 22 November 1740, Egmont Papers, Vol. 14205; Humble Petition of the Poor Distressed Inhabitants of the Province of Georgia to the King or Parliament, 29 December 1740, ibid.

42. Humble Petition . . . to the King or Parliament, 29 December 1740, ibid.

43. First quote, John Fallowfield to Trustees, 1 January 1741, ibid., Vol. 14205. Fallowfield, though a bailiff, was among those who signed the petition to the King or Parliament. Second quote, John Fallowfield to Trustees, 27 July 1742, ibid., Vol. 14206.

44. Clarence L. Ver Steeg, ed., *A True and Historical Narrative* (Athens, 1960), pp. ix–xxxi. The debates in Parliament touched off by the memorials and petitions from discontented Georgia settlers are found in Leo F. Stock, ed., *Proceedings and Debates of the British Parliaments respecting North America* (Washington, D.C., 1941), Vol. 5, 1739–1754, passim. The best analyses of these debates are Richard S. Dunn, "The Trustees of Georgia and the House of Commons, 1732–1752" in *William and Mary Quarterly*, XI, no. 2 (1954), 551–565 and Taylor, *Georgia Plan*, 143–227.

FOUR—*Slaves, Slavery, and the Genesis of the Plantation System in South Carolina*

1. The materials and the concepts for this essay grew out of an extensive investigation of the primary, largely manuscript, sources developed over a decade. I have had the good fortune to be able to consult the recent book of Converse D. Clowse, *Economic Beginnings in Colonial South Carolina, 1670–1730* (Columbia, 1971), whose own pioneering studies on early Caro-

lina trade fill an immense gap and enable scholars to be more precise in their generalizations. Bringing together the researches for this essay in its present form was originally initiated at the Institute for Advanced Study at Princeton when I was appointed a Visiting Member in 1967–1968. I am grateful to the Institute for its generosity. Many of the conclusions offered in this essay were originally advanced in the spring of 1968 in the Columbia Seminar in Early American History.

2. The most widely consulted study is that of Winthrop D. Jordan, *White Over Black: American Attitudes toward the Negro, 1550–1812* (Chapel Hill, 1968), but other essays are important, such as that of Oscar and Mary Handlin, "Origins of the Southern Labor System," in *William and Mary College Quarterly*, VII (1950), 199–223. Peter H. Wood's *Black Majority: Negroes in Colonial South Carolina from 1670 through the Stono Rebellion* (New York, 1974) appeared after this manuscript was at the publisher, so its findings could not be incorporated. Scholars of the period will find *Black Majority* an important work to consult.

3. [Thomas Nairne], "A Letter from South Carolina; Giving an Account of the Soil, Air, Product, Trade, Government, Laws, Religion, People, Military Strength, etc., of that Province, together with the Manner and Necessary Changes of Settling a Plantation There, and the Annual Profit it will Produce," Written by a Swiss Gentleman to His Friend at Bern, Printed for A. Baldwin, near the Oxford-Arms in Warwich-Lane, 1710 (London).

4. I am indebted to Wendell D. Garrett who supplied me with this valuable quote after attending my seminar given at Columbia University in 1968.

5. Governor Charles Craven to Secretary Lord Townshend, 23 May 1715, printed in *North Carolina Colonial Records*, II, 177–179; Proprietors to Board of Trade, 27 July 1716, *Records in the British Public Record Office Relating to South Carolina*, VI, 230–231 (hereafter cited as BPRO). A contemporary wrote: "In the mean time the Publick is put to a vast Expence, a standing army is now raising to consist of 600 whites and 400 Negroes at 4£ per month." John Tate to Board of Trade, Charles Town, 20 September 1715, BPRO, VI, 126–127.

6. Memorial of Joseph Boone and Richard Beresford, Agents for the Commons House of Assembly to the Lords Commissioners of Trade and Plantations, Received 5 December 1716, BPRO, VI, 261–269, printed in *Calendar of State Papers, Colonial Series*, XXIX, 215–218 (hereafter cited as CSP). Notice the use of "husbands and wives," one of many pieces of evidence in the eighteenth-century colonies indicating that black families did exist and were identified as such by name and relationship.

7. Robert L. Meriwether, *The Expansion of South Carolina, 1729–65* (Kingsport, Tenn., 1940).

8. My figures are extrapolated from various scattered reports and letters covering the period from early settlements until the second decade of the eighteenth century. No single set of figures can be presumed to be accurate; those judged to be closest to the mark follow a curve that bears some relationship to benchmark reports such as that of Nathaniel Johnson, Thomas Broughton, Robert Gibbs, George Smith and Richard Beresford to the Proprietors, 17 September 1708, A. S. Salley, indexer, *Records in the British*

Public Record Office Relating to South Carolina, pages 203–210. Although our conclusions do not always agree, Converse Clowse provides a thorough demographic analysis for this period in *Economic Beginnings*, chap. 5, entitled "Improving Prospects, 1690–1705." I have been fortunate that Richard S. Dunn made the original sources of the Barbadoes Census of c. 1680 available to me in 1968. His exceptionally thoughtful article on the incoming Barbadians entitled "The English Sugar Islands and the Founding of South Carolina" is found in the *South Carolina Historical Magazine*, LXXII (April 1971), 81–93.

9. Almon Wheeler Lauber, *Indian Slavery in Colonial Times Within the Present Limits of the United States*, published in *Studies in History, Economics, and Public Law* (New York, 1913), see in particular pp. 105–108. Verner Crane's invaluable study, *The Southern Frontier, 1670–1732* (Durham, 1928), pp. 112–114, proves that no less than 75 Indian slaves were exported in 1712–1713 and 308 in 1716.

10. Thomas Nairne to [? the Earl of Sunderland] in *CSP*, June, 1708–1709, p. 422.

11. Both quotes cited in Crane, *Southern Frontier*, p. 110.

12. The impact of the Indian trade on colonial security and on the culture of Native Americans was profound. English goods transformed Indian life. English trade gave the Native American his blanket, his sharp metal tomahawk, his knife, and his large brass cooking kettle, each item identified later in the popular imagination as indigenous to the Indian. The trade brought an improvement in weapons used by Indians, and, ironically, it even provided warriors with war paint. More important, the Native American became so dependent upon the trade that it became an addiction as pernicious as drugs.

13. Quoted in Crane, *Southern Frontier*, p. 108.

14. For the first and third quotes, A. S. Salley, Jr., ed., *Narratives of Early Carolina, 1650–1708* (New York, 1911), pp. 171, 172; for second quote [Thomas Nairne], *A Letter From South Carolina . . .* , p. 13.

15. Thomas Cooper, ed., *The Statutes at Large of South Carolina* (Columbia, 1837), II, 55–56.

16. Memorial of Joseph Boone and Richard Beresford, Received 22 June 1716, in BPRO, VI, 173–174.

17. Memorial of Joseph Boone and Richard Beresford, Received 22 February 1717, in BPRO, VII, 5–8; Journal of the Board of Trade, 16 July 1715, in BPRO, pp. 137–139.

18. Enclosure of Memorial to the Board of Trade by Joseph Boone and Richard Beresford, Agents for the Province of South Carolina, Received 22 June 1716, BPRO, pp. 173–174.

19. Lewis C. Gray, *History of Agriculture in the Southern United States to 1860* (reprint, New York, 1941), II, 1021.

20. "Letter of Edward Randolph to the Board of Trade, 1699," in Salley, ed., *Narratives of Early Carolina*, pp. 204–210; for the quote, p. 207.

21. Eleanor L. Lord, *Industrial Experiments in the British Colonies of North America*, in *Johns Hopkins University Studies*, Extra Volume XVII (Baltimore, 1898), 64–65.

22. Francis Yonge to Board of Trade, Received 5 February 1723, in BPRO, pp. 2–10, but especially pp. 3–4. Yonge claims the Carolina manufacture of naval stores drastically reduced their costs for Britain. This particular letter provides detail which traces the temporary end of ranch farming and the rise of rice and particularly naval stores to preeminence.

23. Memorial of Joseph Boone and Richard Beresford to Board of Trade, Received 22 June 1716, BPRO, pp. 173–174.

24. I have made use of these figures in manuscript form, but the discriminating, precise analysis of them by Clowse, *Economic Beginnings*, Appendix, Table III, supersedes all previous studies. In a Report to the Board of Trade by Joseph Boone and John Barnwell, Agents of South Carolina, Received 23 August 1720, BPRO, VIII, 65, they reported that in 1720 the colony would be exporting 16,000 tons of rice and 70,000 barrels of pitch, tar, and turpentine. Clowse's figures indicate that this goal was not reached, although more than 60,000 barrels of naval stores were shipped out of Charleston in 1725.

25. Rice producers, whose crop season extended from April-May to September-October, had already learned to use their slaves for the off-season production of naval stores.

26. Governor Robert Johnson to Board of Trade, 12 January 1719, Received 27 April 1720, BPRO, VII, 246–248.

27. Joseph Boone and John Barnwell, Response to Queries of the Board of Trade, Received 23 August 1720, BPRO, VIII, 67. Their response concluded with the warning that the increase in slave importation was "to the endangering [of] the Province." After 1724, the year of the largest quantity of exports of pitch and tar and also the year the subsidy ended, the naval stores industry in South Carolina declined. In the 1730s North Carolina became the center of the industry in North America, a position it was to retain for the remainder of the colonial period. Logical reasons explain the change: the ending of the subsidy; the great forests of longleaf pine located in North Carolina compared with the dwindling supply in South Carolina; and the recovery of rice production in South Carolina. Despite the reduced importance of the production of naval stores in South Carolina, its role in the development of the plantation system in South Carolina during the second decade of the eighteenth century was never erased.

28. Obviously, this calculation depends for its accuracy upon the figure selected as an approximation of the population. Scholars may debate my choice. For 1708, the estimate selected for total population was 9,580 persons, of whom some 4,100 were slaves. For 1721, the estimate selected for total population was 19,600 persons, of whom some 11,800 were slaves.

Index